FOREWORD

The collection of "Everything Will Be Okay" travel phrasebooks published by T&P Books is designed for people traveling abroad for tourism and business. The phrasebooks contain what matters most - the essentials for basic communication. This is an indispensable set of phrases to "survive" while abroad.

This phrasebook will help you in most cases where you need to ask something, get directions, find out how much something costs, etc. It can also resolve difficult communication situations where gestures just won't help.

This book contains a lot of phrases that have been grouped according to the most relevant topics. The edition also includes a small vocabulary that contains roughly 3,000 of the most frequently used words. Another section of the phrasebook provides a gastronomical dictionary that may help you order food at a restaurant or buy groceries at the store.

Take "Everything Will Be Okay" phrasebook with you on the road and you'll have an irreplaceable traveling companion who will help you find your way out of any situation and teach you to not fear speaking with foreigners.

TABLE OF CONTENTS

T&P Books Publishing

Travel phrasebooks collection
«Everything Will Be Okay!»

T&P Books Publishing

PHRASEBOOK

— FRENCH —

By Andrey Taranov

THE MOST IMPORTANT PHRASES

This phrasebook contains
the most important
phrases and questions
for basic communication
Everything you need
to survive overseas

T&P BOOKS

Phrasebook + 3000-word dictionary

English-French phrasebook & topical vocabulary

By Andrey Taranov

The collection of "Everything Will Be Okay" travel phrasebooks published by T&P Books is designed for people traveling abroad for tourism and business. The phrasebooks contain what matters most - the essentials for basic communication. This is an indispensable set of phrases to "survive" while abroad.

This book also includes a small topical vocabulary that contains roughly 3,000 of the most frequently used words. Another section of the phrasebook provides a gastronomical dictionary that may help you order food at a restaurant or buy groceries at the store.

T&P Books Publishing
www.tpbooks.com

ISBN: 978-1-78492-459-1

This book is also available in E-book formats.
Please visit www.tpbooks.com or the major online bookstores.

PRONUNCIATION

Letter	French example	T&P phonetic alphabet	English example

Vowels

Letter	French example	T&P phonetic alphabet	English example
A a	cravate	[a]	shorter than in ask
E e	mer	[ɛ]	man, bad
I i [1]	hier	[j]	yes, New York
I i [2]	musique	[i]	shorter than in feet
O o	porte	[o], [ɔ]	drop, baught
U u	rue	[y]	fuel, tuna
Y y [3]	yacht	[j]	yes, New York
Y y [4]	type	[i]	shorter than in feet

Consonants

Letter	French example	T&P phonetic alphabet	English example
B b	robe	[b]	baby, book
C c [5]	place	[s]	city, boss
C c [6]	canard	[k]	clock, kiss
Ç ç	leçon	[s]	city, boss
D d	disque	[d]	day, doctor
F f	femme	[f]	face, food
G g [7]	page	[ʒ]	forge, pleasure
G g [8]	gare	[g]	game, gold
H h	héros	[h]	silent [h]
J j	jour	[ʒ]	forge, pleasure
K k	kilo	[k]	clock, kiss
L l	aller	[l]	lace, people
M m	maison	[m]	magic, milk
N n	nom	[n]	name, normal
P p	papier	[p]	pencil, private
Q q	cinq	[k]	clock, kiss
R r	mars	[r]	rolled [r]
S s [9]	raison	[z]	zebra, please
S s [10]	sac	[s]	city, boss
T t	table	[t]	tourist, trip
V v	verre	[v]	very, river
W w	Taïwan	[w]	vase, winter

Letter	French example	T&P phonetic alphabet	English example
X x [11]	expliquer	[ks]	box, taxi
X x [12]	exact	[gz]	exam, exact
X x [13]	dix	[s]	city, boss
X x [14]	dixième	[z]	zebra, please
Z z	zéro	[z]	zebra, please

Combinations of letters

ai	faire	[ɛ]	man, bad
au	faute	[o], [o:]	floor, doctor
ay	payer	[eɪ]	age, today
ei	treize	[ɛ]	man, bad
eau	eau	[o], [o:]	floor, doctor
eu	beurre	[ø]	eternal, church
œ	œil	[ø]	eternal, church
œu	cœur	[ø:]	first, thirsty
ou	nous	[u]	book
oi	noir	[wa]	watt, white
oy	voyage	[wa]	watt, white
qu	quartier	[k]	clock, kiss

ch	chat	[ʃ]	machine, shark
th	thé	[t]	tourist, trip
ph	photo	[f]	face, food
gu [15]	guerre	[g]	game, gold
ge [16]	géographie	[ʒ]	forge, pleasure
gn	ligne	[ɲ]	canyon, new
on, om	maison, nom	[ɔ̃]	strong

Comments

[1] before vowels
[2] elsewhere
[3] before vowels
[4] elsewhere
[5] before e, i, y
[6] elsewhere
[7] before e, i, y
[8] elsewhere
[9] between two vowels

[10] elsewhere
[11] most of cases
[12] rarely
[13] in dix, six, soixante
[14] in dixième, sixième
[15] before e, i, u
[16] before a, o, y

LIST OF ABBREVIATIONS

English abbreviations

ab.	-	about
adj	-	adjective
adv	-	adverb
anim.	-	animate
as adj	-	attributive noun used as adjective
e.g.	-	for example
etc.	-	et cetera
fam.	-	familiar
fem.	-	feminine
form.	-	formal
inanim.	-	inanimate
masc.	-	masculine
math	-	mathematics
mil.	-	military
n	-	noun
pl	-	plural
pron.	-	pronoun
sb	-	somebody
sing.	-	singular
sth	-	something
v aux	-	auxiliary verb
vi	-	intransitive verb
vi, vt	-	intransitive, transitive verb
vt	-	transitive verb

French abbreviations

adj	-	adjective
adv	-	adverb
conj	-	conjunction
etc.	-	et cetera
f	-	feminine noun
f pl	-	feminine plural
m	-	masculine noun
m pl	-	masculine plural
m, f	-	masculine, feminine

pl	-	plural
prep	-	preposition
pron	-	pronoun
v aux	-	auxiliary verb
v imp	-	impersonnel verb
vi	-	intransitive verb
vi, vt	-	intransitive, transitive verb
vp	-	pronominal verb
vt	-	transitive verb

T&P BOOKS

FRENCH PHRASEBOOK

This section contains
important phrases that may
come in handy in various
real-life situations.
The phrasebook will help
you ask for directions, clarify
a price, buy tickets, and
order food at a restaurant

T&P Books Publishing

PHRASEBOOK CONTENTS

T&P Books Publishing

The bare minimum

Excuse me, …	**Excusez-moi, …** [ɛkskyze mwa, …]
Hello.	**Bonjour** [bɔ̃ʒuːr]
Thank you.	**Merci** [mɛrsi]
Good bye.	**Au revoir** [o rəvwaːr]
Yes.	**Oui** [wi]
No.	**Non** [nɔ̃]
I don't know.	**Je ne sais pas.** [ʒə nə sɛ pɑ]
Where? | Where to? | When?	**Où? | Où? | Quand?** [u? | u? | kɑ̃?]
I need …	**J'ai besoin de …** [ʒe bəzwɛ̃ də …]
I want …	**Je veux …** [ʒə vø …]
Do you have …?	**Avez-vous … ?** [ave vu …?]
Is there a … here?	**Est-ce qu'il y a … ici?** [ɛs kilja … isi?]
May I …?	**Puis-je … ?** [pɥiʒ …?]
…, please (polite request)	**…, s'il vous plaît** […, sil vu plɛ]
I'm looking for …	**Je cherche …** [ʒə ʃɛrʃ …]
restroom	**les toilettes** [le twalɛt]
ATM	**un distributeur** [œ̃ distribytœːr]
pharmacy (drugstore)	**une pharmacie** [yn farmasi]
hospital	**l'hôpital** [lɔpital]
police station	**le commissariat de police** [lə kɔmisarja də polis]
subway	**une station de métro** [yn stasjɔ̃ də metro]

taxi	**un taxi** [œ̃ taksi]
train station	**la gare** [la gar]

My name is ...	**Je m'appelle ...** [ʒə mapɛl ...]
What's your name?	**Comment vous appelez-vous?** [kɔmɑ̃ vuzaple-vu?]
Could you please help me?	**Aidez-moi, s'il vous plaît.** [ɛde-mwa, sil vu plɛ]
I've got a problem.	**J'ai un problème.** [ʒe œ̃ prɔblɛm]
I don't feel well.	**Je ne me sens pas bien.** [ʒə nə me sɑ̃ pɑ bjɛ̃]
Call an ambulance!	**Appelez une ambulance!** [aple yn ɑ̃bylɑ̃:s!]
May I make a call?	**Puis-je faire un appel?** [pɥiʒ fɛr œn apɛl?]

I'm sorry.	**Excusez-moi.** [ɛkskyze mwa]
You're welcome.	**Je vous en prie.** [ʒə vuzɑ̃pri]

I, me	**je, moi** [ʒə, mwa]
you (inform.)	**tu, toi** [ty, twa]
he	**il** [il]
she	**elle** [ɛl]
they (masc.)	**ils** [il]
they (fem.)	**elles** [ɛl]
we	**nous** [nu]
you (pl)	**vous** [vu]
you (sg, form.)	**Vous** [vu]

ENTRANCE	**ENTRÉE** [ɑ̃tre]
EXIT	**SORTIE** [sɔrti]
OUT OF ORDER	**HORS SERVICE | EN PANNE** [ɔr sɛrvis | ɑ̃ pan]
CLOSED	**FERMÉ** [fɛrme]

OPEN

OUVERT
[uvɛr]

FOR WOMEN

POUR LES FEMMES
[pur le fam]

FOR MEN

POUR LES HOMMES
[pur le zɔm]

Questions

Where?	**Où?** [u?]
Where to?	**Où?** [u?]
Where from?	**D'où?** [du?]
Why?	**Pourquoi?** [purkwa?]
For what reason?	**Pour quelle raison?** [pur kɛl rɛzɔ̃?]
When?	**Quand?** [kɑ̃?]

How long?	**Combien de temps?** [kɔ̃bjɛ̃ də tɑ̃?]
At what time?	**À quelle heure?** [a kɛl œ:r?]
How much?	**C'est combien?** [sɛ kɔ̃bjɛ̃?]
Do you have ...?	**Avez-vous ... ?** [ave vu ...?]
Where is ...?	**Où est ..., s'il vous plaît?** [u ɛ ..., sil vu plɛ?]

What time is it?	**Quelle heure est-il?** [kɛl œr ɛ-til?]
May I make a call?	**Puis-je faire un appel?** [pɥiʒ fɛr œn apɛl?]
Who's there?	**Qui est là?** [ki ɛ la?]
Can I smoke here?	**Puis-je fumer ici?** [pɥiʒ fyme isi?]
May I ...?	**Puis-je ...?** [pɥiʒ ...?]

Needs

I'd like ...	**Je voudrais ...** [ʒə vudrɛ ...]
I don't want ...	**Je ne veux pas ...** [ʒə nə vø pɑ ...]
I'm thirsty.	**J'ai soif.** [ʒe swaf]
I want to sleep.	**Je veux dormir.** [ʒə vø dɔrmi:r]

I want ...	**Je veux ...** [ʒə vø ...]
to wash up	**me laver** [mə lave]
to brush my teeth	**brosser mes dents** [brɔse me dɑ̃]
to rest a while	**me reposer un instant** [mə rəpoze œn ɛ̃stɑ̃]
to change my clothes	**changer de vêtements** [ʃɑ̃ʒe də vɛtmɑ̃]

to go back to the hotel	**retourner à l'hôtel** [rəturne a lotɛl]
to buy ...	**acheter ...** [aʃte ...]
to go to ...	**aller à ...** [ale a ...]
to visit ...	**visiter ...** [vizite ...]
to meet with ...	**rencontrer ...** [rɑ̃kɔ̃tre ...]
to make a call	**faire un appel** [fɛr œn apɛl]

I'm tired.	**Je suis fatigué /fatiguée/** [ʒə sɥi fatige]
We are tired.	**Nous sommes fatigués /fatiguées/** [nu sɔm fatige]
I'm cold.	**J'ai froid.** [ʒe frwɑ]
I'm hot.	**J'ai chaud.** [ʒe ʃo]
I'm OK.	**Je suis bien.** [ʒə sɥi bjɛ̃]

I need to make a call.

Il me faut faire un appel.
[il mə fo fɛr œn apɛl]

I need to go to the restroom.

J'ai besoin d'aller aux toilettes.
[ʒe bəzwɛ̃ dale o twalɛt]

I have to go.

Il faut que j'aille.
[il fo kə ʒaj]

I have to go now.

Je dois partir maintenant.
[ʒə dwa partir mɛ̃tnɑ̃]

Asking for directions

Excuse me, ...	**Excusez-moi, ...** [ɛkskyze mwa, ...]
Where is ...?	**Où est ..., s'il vous plaît?** [u ɛ ..., sil vu plɛ?]
Which way is ...?	**Dans quelle direction est ... ?** [dɑ̃ kɛl dirɛksjɔ̃ ɛ ... ?]
Could you help me, please?	**Pouvez-vous m'aider, s'il vous plaît?** [puve vu mɛde, sil vu plɛ?]

I'm looking for ...	**Je cherche ...** [ʒə ʃɛrʃ ...]
I'm looking for the exit.	**La sortie, s'il vous plaît?** [la sɔrti, sil vu plɛ?]
I'm going to ...	**Je vais à ...** [ʒə ve a ...]
Am I going the right way to ...?	**C'est la bonne direction pour ...?** [sɛ la bɔn dirɛksjɔ̃ pur ...?]

Is it far?	**C'est loin?** [sɛ lwɛ̃?]
Can I get there on foot?	**Est-ce que je peux y aller à pied?** [ɛskə ʒə pø i ale a pje?]
Can you show me on the map?	**Pouvez-vous me le montrer sur la carte?** [puve vu mə lə mɔ̃tre syr la kart?]
Show me where we are right now.	**Montrez-moi où sommes-nous, s'il vous plaît.** [mɔ̃tre-mwa u sɔm-nu, sil vu plɛ]

Here	**Ici** [isi]
There	**Là-bas** [labɑ]
This way	**Par ici** [par isi]

Turn right.	**Tournez à droite.** [turne a drwat]
Turn left.	**Tournez à gauche.** [turne a goʃ]

first (second, third) turn

**Prenez la première
(deuxième, troisième) rue.**
[prəne la prəmjɛr
(døzjɛm, trwazjɛm) ry]

to the right

à droite
[a drwat]

to the left

à gauche
[a goʃ]

Go straight.

Continuez tout droit.
[kɔ̃tinɥe tu drwa]

Signs

WELCOME!	**BIENVENUE!** [bjɛ̃vny!]
ENTRANCE	**ENTRÉE** [ɑ̃tre]
EXIT	**SORTIE** [sɔrti]

PUSH	**POUSSEZ** [puse]
PULL	**TIREZ** [tire]
OPEN	**OUVERT** [uvɛr]
CLOSED	**FERMÉ** [fɛrme]

FOR WOMEN	**POUR LES FEMMES** [pur le fam]
FOR MEN	**POUR LES HOMMES** [pur le zɔm]
MEN, GENTS	**MESSIEURS (M)** [məsjø]
WOMEN, LADIES	**FEMMES (F)** [fam]

DISCOUNTS	**RABAIS | SOLDES** [rabɛ | sɔld]
SALE	**PROMOTION** [prɔmɔsjɔ̃]
FREE	**GRATUIT** [gratɥi]
NEW!	**NOUVEAU!** [nuvo!]
ATTENTION!	**ATTENTION!** [atɑ̃sjɔ̃!]

NO VACANCIES	**COMPLET** [kɔ̃plɛ]
RESERVED	**RÉSERVÉ** [rezɛrve]
ADMINISTRATION	**ADMINISTRATION** [administrasjɔ̃]
STAFF ONLY	**PERSONNEL SEULEMENT** [pɛrsɔnɛl sœlmɑ̃]

BEWARE OF THE DOG!	**ATTENTION AU CHIEN!** [atɑ̃sjɔ̃ o ʃjɛ̃!]
NO SMOKING!	**NE PAS FUMER!** [nə pɑ fyme!]
DO NOT TOUCH!	**NE PAS TOUCHER!** [nə pɑ tuʃe!]
DANGEROUS	**DANGEREUX** [dɑ̃ʒrø]
DANGER	**DANGER** [dɑ̃ʒe]
HIGH VOLTAGE	**HAUTE TENSION** [ot tɑ̃sjɔ̃]
NO SWIMMING!	**BAIGNADE INTERDITE!** [bɛɲad ɛ̃tɛrdit!]

OUT OF ORDER	**HORS SERVICE	EN PANNE** [ɔr sɛrvis	ɑ̃ pan]
FLAMMABLE	**INFLAMMABLE** [ɛ̃flamabl]
FORBIDDEN	**INTERDIT** [ɛ̃tɛrdi]
NO TRESPASSING!	**ENTRÉE INTERDITE!** [ɑ̃tre ɛ̃tɛrdit!]
WET PAINT	**PEINTURE FRAÎCHE** [pɛ̃tyr frɛʃ]

CLOSED FOR RENOVATIONS	**FERMÉ POUR TRAVAUX** [fɛrme pur travɔ]
WORKS AHEAD	**TRAVAUX EN COURS** [travɔ ɑ̃ kur]
DETOUR	**DÉVIATION** [devjasjɔ̃]

Transportation. General phrases

plane	**avion** [avjɔ̃]
train	**train** [trɛ̃]
bus	**bus, autobus** [bys, otɔbys]
ferry	**ferry** [feri]
taxi	**taxi** [taksi]
car	**voiture** [vwatyr]

schedule	**horaire** [ɔrɛr]
Where can I see the schedule?	**Où puis-je voir l'horaire?** [u pɥiʒ vwar lɔrɛ:r?]
workdays (weekdays)	**jours ouvrables** [ʒur uvrabl]
weekends	**jours non ouvrables** [ʒur nɔn uvrabl]
holidays	**jours fériés** [ʒur ferje]

DEPARTURE	**DÉPART** [depar]
ARRIVAL	**ARRIVÉE** [arive]
DELAYED	**RETARDÉE** [rətarde]
CANCELED	**ANNULÉE** [anyle]

next (train, etc.)	**prochain** [prɔʃɛ̃]
first	**premier** [prəmje]
last	**dernier** [dɛrnje]

When is the next ...?	**À quelle heure est le prochain ...?** [a kɛl œr ɛ lə prɔʃɛ̃ ...?]
When is the first ...?	**À quelle heure est le premier ...?** [a kɛl œr ɛ lə prəmje ...?]

When is the last ...?

À quelle heure est le dernier ...?
[a kɛl œr ɛ lə dɛrnje ...?]

transfer (change of trains, etc.)

correspondance
[kɔrɛspõdãs]

to make a transfer

prendre la correspondance
[prãdr la kɔrɛspõdãs]

Do I need to make a transfer?

Dois-je prendre la correspondance?
[dwaʒ prãdr la kɔrɛspõdãs?]

Buying tickets

Where can I buy tickets?	**Où puis-je acheter des billets?** [u pɥiʒ aʃte de bijɛ?]
ticket	**billet** [bijɛ]
to buy a ticket	**acheter un billet** [aʃte œ̃ bijɛ]
ticket price	**le prix d'un billet** [lə pri dœ̃ bijɛ]

Where to?	**Pour aller où?** [pur ale u?]
To what station?	**Quelle destination?** [kɛl dɛstinasjɔ̃?]
I need ...	**Je voudrais ...** [ʒə vudrɛ ...]
one ticket	**un billet** [œ̃ bijɛ]
two tickets	**deux billets** [dø bijɛ]
three tickets	**trois billets** [trwɑ bijɛ]

one-way	**aller simple** [ale sɛ̃pl]
round-trip	**aller-retour** [ale-rətur]
first class	**première classe** [prəmjɛr klɑs]
second class	**classe économique** [klɑs ekɔnɔmik]

today	**aujourd'hui** [oʒurdɥi]
tomorrow	**demain** [dəmɛ̃]
the day after tomorrow	**après-demain** [aprɛdmɛ̃]
in the morning	**dans la matinée** [dɑ̃ la matine]
in the afternoon	**l'après-midi** [laprɛmidi]
in the evening	**dans la soirée** [dɑ̃ la sware]

aisle seat

siège côté couloir
[sjɛʒ kote kulwar]

window seat

siège côté fenêtre
[sjɛʒ kote fənɛtr]

How much?

C'est combien?
[sɛ kɔ̃bjɛ̃?]

Can I pay by credit card?

Puis-je payer avec la carte?
[pɥiʒ peje avɛk la kart?]

Bus

bus	**bus, autobus** [otɔbys]
intercity bus	**autocar** [otɔkar]
bus stop	**arrêt d'autobus** [arɛ dotɔbys]
Where's the nearest bus stop?	**Où est l'arrêt d'autobus** **le plus proche?** [u ɛ larɛ dotɔbys lə ply prɔʃ?]

number (bus ~, etc.)	**numéro** [nymero]
Which bus do I take to get to …?	**Quel bus dois-je prendre** **pour aller à …?** [kɛl bys dwaʒ prɑ̃dr pur ale a …?]
Does this bus go to …?	**Est-ce que ce bus va à …?** [ɛskə sə bys va a …?]
How frequent are the buses?	**L'autobus passe tous les combien?** [lotɔbys pɑs tu le kɔ̃bjɛ̃?]

every 15 minutes	**chaque quart d'heure** [ʃak kar dœr]
every half hour	**chaque demi-heure** [ʃak dəmiœr]
every hour	**chaque heure** [ʃak œr]
several times a day	**plusieurs fois par jour** [plyzjœr fwa par ʒur]
… times a day	**… fois par jour** [… fwa par ʒur]

schedule	**horaire** [ɔrɛr]
Where can I see the schedule?	**Où puis-je voir l'horaire?** [u pɥiʒ vwar lɔrɛ:r?]
When is the next bus?	**À quelle heure passe le prochain bus?** [a kɛl œr pɑs lə prɔʃɛ̃ bys?]
When is the first bus?	**À quelle heure passe le premier bus?** [a kɛl œr pɑs lə prəmje bys?]
When is the last bus?	**À quelle heure passe le dernier bus?** [a kɛl œr pɑs lə dɛrnje bys?]

stop

arrêt
[arɛ]

next stop

prochain arrêt
[prɔʃɛn arɛ]

last stop (terminus)

terminus
[tɛrminys]

Stop here, please.

Pouvez-vous arrêter ici, s'il vous plaît.
[puve vu arɛte isi, sil vu plɛ]

Excuse me, this is my stop.

Excusez-moi, c'est mon arrêt.
[ɛkskyze mwa, sɛ mɔ̃n arɛ]

Train

train
train
[trɛ̃]

suburban train
train de banlieue
[trɛ̃ də bɑ̃ljø]

long-distance train
train de grande ligne
[trɛ̃ də grɑ̃d liɲ]

train station
la gare
[la gar]

Excuse me, where is the exit
to the platform?
**Excusez-moi, où est la sortie
vers les quais?**
[ɛkskyze mwa, u ɛ la sɔrti
vɛr le ke?]

Does this train go to ...?
Est-ce que ce train va à ...?
[ɛskə sə trɛ̃ va a ...?]

next train
le prochain train
[lə prɔʃɛ̃ trɛ̃]

When is the next train?
À quelle heure est le prochain train?
[a kɛl œr ɛ lə prɔʃɛ̃ trɛ̃?]

Where can I see the schedule?
Où puis-je voir l'horaire?
[u pɥiʒ vwar lɔrɛːr?]

From which platform?
De quel quai?
[də kɛl ke?]

When does the train arrive in ...?
À quelle heure arrive le train à ...?
[a kɛl œr ariv lə trɛ̃ a ...?]

Please help me.
Pouvez-vous m'aider, s'il vous plaît?
[puve-vu mɛde, sil vu plɛ?]

I'm looking for my seat.
Je cherche ma place.
[ʒə ʃɛrʃ ma plas]

We're looking for our seats.
Nous cherchons nos places.
[nu ʃɛrʃɔ̃ no plas]

My seat is taken.
Ma place est occupée.
[ma plas ɛtokype]

Our seats are taken.
Nos places sont occupées.
[no plas sɔ̃ ɔkype]

I'm sorry but this is my seat.
Excusez-moi, mais c'est ma place.
[ɛkskyze mwa, mɛ sɛ ma plas]

Is this seat taken?
Est-ce que cette place est libre?
[ɛskə sɛt plas ɛ liːbr?]

May I sit here?
Puis-je m'asseoir ici?
[pɥiʒ maswar isi?]

On the train. Dialogue (No ticket)

Ticket, please.

Votre billet, s'il vous plaît.
[vɔtr bijɛ, sil vu plɛ]

I don't have a ticket.

Je n'ai pas de billet.
[ʒə ne pɑ də bijɛ]

I lost my ticket.

J'ai perdu mon billet.
[ʒe pɛrdy mɔ̃ bijɛ]

I forgot my ticket at home.

J'ai oublié mon billet à la maison.
[ʒe ublije mɔ̃ bijɛ a la mɛzɔ̃]

You can buy a ticket from me.

Vous pouvez m'acheter un billet.
[vu puve maʃte œ̃ bijɛ]

You will also have to pay a fine.

Vous devrez aussi payer une amende.
[vu dəvre osi peje yn amɑ̃d]

Okay.

D'accord.
[dakɔ:r]

Where are you going?

Où allez-vous?
[u ale-vu?]

I'm going to ...

Je vais à ...
[ʒə ve a ...]

How much? I don't understand.

Combien? Je ne comprend pas.
[kɔ̃bjɛ̃? ʒə nə kɔ̃prɑ̃ pɑ]

Write it down, please.

Pouvez-vous l'écrire, s'il vous plaît.
[puve vu lekrir, sil vu plɛ]

Okay. Can I pay with a credit card?

D'accord. Puis-je payer avec la carte?
[dakɔ:r. pɥiʒ peje avɛk la kart?]

Yes, you can.

Oui, bien sûr.
[wi, bjɛ̃ sy:r]

Here's your receipt.

Voici votre reçu.
[vwasi vɔtr rəsy]

Sorry about the fine.

Désolé pour l'amende.
[dezɔle pur lamɑ̃:d]

That's okay. It was my fault.

Ça va. C'est de ma faute.
[sa va. sɛ də ma fot]

Enjoy your trip.

Bon voyage.
[bɔ̃ vwaja:ʒ]

Taxi

taxi	**taxi** [taksi]
taxi driver	**chauffeur de taxi** [ʃofœr də taksi]
to catch a taxi	**prendre un taxi** [prɑ̃dr œ̃ taksi]
taxi stand	**arrêt de taxi** [arɛ də taksi]
Where can I get a taxi?	**Où puis-je trouver un taxi?** [u pɥiʒ truve œ̃ taksi?]
to call a taxi	**appeler un taxi** [aple œ̃ taksi]
I need a taxi.	**Il me faut un taxi.** [il mə fo œ̃ taksi]
Right now.	**maintenant** [mɛ̃tnɑ̃]
What is your address (location)?	**Quelle est votre adresse?** [kɛl ɛ vɔtr adrɛs?]
My address is ...	**Mon adresse est ...** [mɔn adrɛs ɛ ...]
Your destination?	**Votre destination?** [vɔtr dɛstinasjɔ̃?]
Excuse me, ...	**Excusez-moi, ...** [ɛkskyze mwa, ...]
Are you available?	**Vous êtes libre ?** [vuzɛt libr?]
How much is it to get to ...?	**Combien ça coûte pour aller à ...?** [kɔ̃bjɛ̃ sa kut pur ale a ...?]
Do you know where it is?	**Vous savez où ça se trouve?** [vu save u sa sə tru:v?]
Airport, please.	**À l'aéroport, s'il vous plaît.** [a laerɔpɔ:r, sil vu plɛ]
Stop here, please.	**Arrêtez ici, s'il vous plaît.** [arɛte isi, sil vu plɛ]
It's not here.	**Ce n'est pas ici.** [sə nɛ pɑ isi]
This is the wrong address.	**C'est la mauvaise adresse.** [sɛ la mɔvɛz adrɛs]
Turn left.	**tournez à gauche** [turne a goʃ]
Turn right.	**tournez à droite** [turne a drwat]

How much do I owe you?	**Combien je vous dois?** [kɔ̃bjɛ̃ ʒə vu dwa?]
I'd like a receipt, please.	**J'aimerais avoir un reçu,** **s'il vous plaît.** [ʒɛmrɛ avwar œ̃ rəsy, sil vu plɛ]
Keep the change.	**Gardez la monnaie.** [garde la mɔnɛ]

Would you please wait for me?	**Attendez-moi, s'il vous plaît ...** [atɑ̃de-mwa, sil vu plɛ ...]
five minutes	**cinq minutes** [sɛ̃k minyt]
ten minutes	**dix minutes** [di minyt]
fifteen minutes	**quinze minutes** [kɛ̃z minyt]
twenty minutes	**vingt minutes** [vɛ̃ minyt]
half an hour	**une demi-heure** [yn dəmiœr]

Hotel

Hello.	**Bonjour.** [bɔ̃ʒu:r]
My name is ...	**Je m'appelle ...** [ʒə mapɛl ...]
I have a reservation.	**J'ai réservé une chambre.** [ʒe rezɛrve yn ʃɑ̃:br]

I need ...	**Je voudrais ...** [ʒə vudrɛ ...]
a single room	**une chambre simple** [yn ʃɑ̃br sɛ̃pl]
a double room	**une chambre double** [yn ʃɑ̃br dubl]
How much is that?	**C'est combien?** [sɛ kɔ̃bjɛ̃?]
That's a bit expensive.	**C'est un peu cher.** [sɛtœ̃pø ʃɛ:r]

Do you have any other options?	**Avez-vous autre chose?** [ave vu otr ʃo:z?]
I'll take it.	**Je vais la prendre.** [ʒə ve la prɑ̃dr]
I'll pay in cash.	**Je vais payer comptant.** [ʒə ve peje kɔ̃tɑ̃]

I've got a problem.	**J'ai un problème.** [ʒe œ̃ prɔblɛm]
My ... is broken.	**... est cassé /cassée/** [... ɛ kase]
My ... is out of order.	**... ne fonctionne pas.** [... nə fɔ̃ksjɔn pɑ]
TV	**la télé ...** [la tele ...]
air conditioning	**air conditionné ...** [ɛr kɔ̃disjɔne ...]
tap	**le robinet ...** [lə rɔbinɛ ...]

shower	**ma douche ...** [ma duʃ ...]
sink	**mon évier ...** [mon evje ...]
safe	**mon coffre-fort ...** [mɔ̃ kɔfr-fɔr ...]

door lock	**la serrure de porte ...** [la seryr də port ...]
electrical outlet	**la prise électrique ...** [la priz elɛktrik ...]
hairdryer	**mon sèche-cheveux ...** [mɔ̃ sɛʃ ʃəvø ...]

I don't have ...	**Je n'ai pas ...** [ʒə ne pɑ ...]
water	**d'eau** [do]
light	**de lumière** [də lymjɛr]
electricity	**d'électricité** [delɛktrisite]

Can you give me ...?	**Pouvez-vous me donner ...?** [puve vu mə dɔne ...?]
a towel	**une serviette** [yn sɛrvjɛt]
a blanket	**une couverture** [yn kuvɛrtyr]
slippers	**des pantoufles** [de pɑ̃tufl]
a robe	**une robe de chambre** [yn rɔb də ʃɑ̃br]
shampoo	**du shampooing** [dy ʃɑ̃pwɛ̃]
soap	**du savon** [dy savɔ̃]

I'd like to change rooms.	**Je voudrais changer ma chambre.** [ʒə vudrɛ ʃɑ̃ʒe ma ʃɑ̃:br]
I can't find my key.	**Je ne trouve pas ma clé.** [ʒə nə truv pɑ ma kle]
Could you open my room, please?	**Pourriez-vous ouvrir ma chambre, s'il vous plaît?** [purje-vu uvrir ma ʃɑ̃:br, sil vu plɛ?]
Who's there?	**Qui est là?** [ki ɛ la?]
Come in!	**Entrez!** [ɑ̃tre!]
Just a minute!	**Une minute!** [yn minyt!]

Not right now, please.	**Pas maintenant, s'il vous plaît.** [pɑ mɛ̃tnɑ̃, sil vu plɛ]
Come to my room, please.	**Pouvez-vous venir à ma chambre, s'il vous plaît.** [puve vu vənir a ma ʃɑ̃:br, sil vu plɛ]

I'd like to order food service.	**J'aimerais avoir le service d'étage.** [ʒɛmrɛ avwar lə sɛrvis deta:ʒ]
My room number is ...	**Mon numéro de chambre est le ...** [mɔ̃ nymero də ʃɑ̃br ɛ lə ...]

I'm leaving ...	**Je pars ...** [ʒə par ...]
We're leaving ...	**Nous partons ...** [nu partɔ̃ ...]
right now	**maintenant** [mɛ̃tnɑ̃]
this afternoon	**cet après-midi** [sɛt aprɛmidi]
tonight	**ce soir** [sə swar]
tomorrow	**demain** [dəmɛ̃]
tomorrow morning	**demain matin** [dəmɛ̃ matɛ̃]
tomorrow evening	**demain après-midi** [dəmɛ̃ aprɛmidi]
the day after tomorrow	**après-demain** [aprɛdmɛ̃]

I'd like to pay.	**Je voudrais régler mon compte.** [ʒə vudrɛ regle mɔ̃ kɔ̃:t]
Everything was wonderful.	**Tout était merveilleux.** [tutetɛ mɛrvɛjø]
Where can I get a taxi?	**Où puis-je trouver un taxi?** [u pɥiʒ truve œ̃ taksi?]
Would you call a taxi for me, please?	**Pourriez-vous m'appeler un taxi, s'il vous plaît?** [purje-vu maple œ̃ taksi, sil vu plɛ?]

Restaurant

Can I look at the menu, please?

Table for one.

There are two (three, four) of us.

Puis-je voir le menu, s'il vous plaît?
[pɥiʒ vwar lə məny, sil vu plɛ?]
Une table pour une personne.
[yn tabl pur yn pɛrsɔn]
Nous sommes deux (trois, quatre).
[nu sɔm dø (trwɑ, katr)]

Smoking

No smoking

Excuse me! (addressing a waiter)

menu

wine list

The menu, please.

Fumeurs
[fymœr]
Non-fumeurs
[nɔ̃-fymœr]
S'il vous plaît!
[sil vu plɛ!]
menu
[məny]
carte des vins
[kart de vɛ̃]
Le menu, s'il vous plaît.
[lə məny, sil vu plɛ]

Are you ready to order?

What will you have?

I'll have ...

Êtes-vous prêts à commander?
[ɛt-vu prɛ a kɔmɑ̃de?]
Qu'allez-vous prendre?
[kale-vu prɑ̃dr?]
Je vais prendre ...
[ʒə ve prɑ̃dr ...]

I'm a vegetarian.

meat

fish

vegetables

Do you have vegetarian dishes?

I don't eat pork.

He /she/ doesn't eat meat.

I am allergic to ...

Je suis végétarien.
[ʒə sɥi veʒetarjɛ̃]
viande
[vjɑ̃d]
poisson
[pwasɔ̃]
légumes
[legym]
Avez-vous des plats végétariens?
[ave vu de pla veʒetarjɛ̃?]
Je ne mange pas de porc.
[ʒə nə mɑ̃ʒ pa də pɔ:r]
Il /elle/ ne mange pas de viande.
[il /ɛl/ nə mɑ̃ʒ pa də vjɑ̃:d]
Je suis allergique à ...
[ʒə sɥi alɛrʒik a ...]

Would you please bring me …	**Pourriez-vous m'apporter …, s'il vous plaît.** [purje-vu maporte … , sil vu plɛ]
salt | pepper | sugar	**le sel | le poivre | du sucre** [lə sɛl | lə pwavr | dy sykr]
coffee | tea | dessert	**un café | un thé | un dessert** [œ̃ kafe | œ̃ te | œ̃ desɛr]
water | sparkling | plain	**de l'eau | gazeuse | plate** [də lo | gazøz | plat]
a spoon | fork | knife	**une cuillère | une fourchette | un couteau** [yn kɥijɛr | yn furʃɛt | œ̃ kuto]
a plate | napkin	**une assiette | une serviette** [yn asjɛt | yn sɛrvjɛt]

Enjoy your meal!	**Bon appétit!** [bɔn apeti!]
One more, please.	**Un de plus, s'il vous plaît.** [œ̃ də plys, sil vu plɛ]
It was very delicious.	**C'était délicieux.** [setɛ delisjø]

check | change | tip	**l'addition | de la monnaie | le pourboire** [ladisjɔ̃ | də la mɔnɛ | lə purbwar]

Check, please. (Could I have the check, please?)	**L'addition, s'il vous plaît.** [ladisjɔ̃, sil vu plɛ]
Can I pay by credit card?	**Puis-je payer avec la carte?** [pɥiʒ peje avɛk la kart?]
I'm sorry, there's a mistake here.	**Excusez-moi, je crois qu'il y a une erreur ici.** [ɛkskyze mwa, ʒə krwa kilja yn ɛrœr isi]

Shopping

Can I help you?	**Est-ce que je peux vous aider?** [ɛskə ʒə pø vuzɛde?]
Do you have ...?	**Avez-vous ... ?** [ave vu ...?]
I'm looking for ...	**Je cherche ...** [ʒə ʃɛrʃ ...]
I need ...	**Il me faut ...** [il mə fo ...]

I'm just looking.	**Je regarde seulement, merci.** [ʒə rəgard sœlmã, mɛrsi]
We're just looking.	**Nous regardons seulement, merci.** [nu rəgardõ sœlmã, mɛrsi]
I'll come back later.	**Je reviendrai plus tard.** [ʒə rəvjɛ̃dre ply ta:r]
We'll come back later.	**On reviendra plus tard.** [õ rəvjɛ̃dra ply ta:r]
discounts | sale	**Rabais | Soldes** [rabɛ | sɔld]

Would you please show me ...	**Montrez-moi, s'il vous plaît ...** [mõtre-mwa, sil vu plɛ ...]
Would you please give me ...	**Donnez-moi, s'il vous plaît ...** [dɔne-mwa, sil vu plɛ ...]
Can I try it on?	**Est-ce que je peux l'essayer?** [ɛskə ʒə pø lesɛje?]
Excuse me, where's the fitting room?	**Excusez-moi, où est la cabine d'essayage?** [ɛkskyze mwa, u ɛ la kabin desɛja:ʒ?]
Which color would you like?	**Quelle couleur aimeriez-vous?** [kɛl kulœr ɛmərje-vu?]
size | length	**taille | longueur** [taj | lõgœr]
How does it fit?	**Est-ce que la taille convient ?** [ɛskə la taj kõvjɛ̃?]

How much is it?	**Combien ça coûte?** [kõbjɛ̃ sa kut?]
That's too expensive.	**C'est trop cher.** [sɛ tro ʃɛ:r]
I'll take it.	**Je vais le prendre.** [ʒə ve lə prãdr]

Excuse me, where do I pay?

Excusez-moi, où est la caisse?
[ɛkskyze mwa, u ɛ la kɛs?]

Will you pay in cash or credit card?

Payerez-vous comptant ou par carte de crédit?
[pɛjre-vu kɔ̃tɑ̃ u par kart də kredi?]

In cash | with credit card

Comptant | par carte de crédit
[kɔ̃tɑ̃ | par kart də kredi]

Do you want the receipt?

Voulez-vous un reçu?
[vule vu œ̃ rəsy?]

Yes, please.

Oui, s'il vous plaît.
[wi, sil vu plɛ]

No, it's OK.

Non, ce n'est pas nécessaire.
[nɔ̃, sə nɛ pɑ nesesɛ:r]

Thank you. Have a nice day!

Merci. Bonne journée!
[mɛrsi. bɔn ʒurne!]

In town

Excuse me, please.	**Excusez-moi, …** [ɛkskyze mwa, …]
I'm looking for …	**Je cherche …** [ʒə ʃɛrʃ …]
the subway	**le métro** [lə metro]
my hotel	**mon hôtel** [mɔn otɛl]
the movie theater	**le cinéma** [lə sinema]
a taxi stand	**un arrêt de taxi** [œn arɛ də taksi]

an ATM	**un distributeur** [œ̃ distribytœ:r]
a foreign exchange office	**un bureau de change** [œ̃ byro də ʃɑ̃ʒ]
an internet café	**un café internet** [œ̃ kafe ɛ̃tɛrnɛt]
… street	**la rue …** [la ry …]
this place	**cette place-ci** [sɛt plas-si]

Do you know where … is?	**Savez-vous où se trouve …?** [save vu u sə truv …?]
Which street is this?	**Quelle est cette rue?** [kɛl ɛ sɛt ry?]
Show me where we are right now.	**Montrez-moi où sommes-nous, s'il vous plaît.** [mɔ̃tre-mwa u sɔm-nu, sil vu plɛ]
Can I get there on foot?	**Est-ce que je peux y aller à pied?** [ɛskə ʒə pø i ale a pje?]
Do you have a map of the city?	**Avez-vous une carte de la ville?** [ave vu yn kart də la vil?]

How much is a ticket to get in?	**C'est combien pour un ticket?** [sɛ kɔ̃bjɛ̃ pur œ̃ tikɛ?]
Can I take pictures here?	**Est-ce que je peux faire des photos?** [ɛskə ʒə pø fɛr de fɔto?]
Are you open?	**Êtes-vous ouvert?** [ɛt-vu uvɛ:r?]

When do you open?

À quelle heure ouvrez-vous?
[a kɛl œr uvre-vu?]

When do you close?

À quelle heure fermez-vous?
[a kɛl œr fɛrme-vu?]

Money

money	**argent** [arʒɑ̃]
cash	**argent liquide** [arʒɑ̃ likid]
paper money	**des billets** [de bijɛ]
loose change	**petite monnaie** [pətit mɔnɛ]
check	change	tip	**l'addition	de la monnaie |** **le pourboire** [ladisjɔ̃	də la mɔnɛ | lə purbwar]
credit card	**carte de crédit** [kart də kredi]
wallet	**portefeuille** [pɔrtəfœj]
to buy	**acheter** [aʃte]
to pay	**payer** [peje]
fine	**amende** [amɑ̃d]
free	**gratuit** [gratɥi]
Where can I buy ...?	**Où puis-je acheter ... ?** [u pɥiʒ aʃte ...?]
Is the bank open now?	**Est-ce que la banque est ouverte** **en ce moment?** [ɛskə la bɑ̃k ɛtuvɛrt ɑ̃ sə mɔmɑ̃?]
When does it open?	**À quelle heure ouvre-t-elle?** [a kɛl œr uvr-tɛl?]
When does it close?	**À quelle heure ferme-t-elle?** [a kɛl œr fɛrm-tɛl?]
How much?	**C'est combien?** [sɛ kɔ̃bjɛ̃?]
How much is this?	**Combien ça coûte?** [kɔ̃bjɛ̃ sa kut?]
That's too expensive.	**C'est trop cher.** [sɛ tro ʃɛːr]

Excuse me, where do I pay?	**Excusez-moi, où est la caisse?** [ɛkskyze mwa, u ɛ la kɛs?]
Check, please.	**L'addition, s'il vous plaît.** [ladisjɔ̃, sil vu plɛ]
Can I pay by credit card?	**Puis-je payer avec la carte?** [pɥiʒ peje avɛk la kart?]
Is there an ATM here?	**Est-ce qu'il y a un distributeur ici?** [ɛskilja œ̃ distribytœːr isi?]
I'm looking for an ATM.	**Je cherche un distributeur.** [ʒə ʃɛrʃ œ̃ distribytœːr]

I'm looking for a foreign exchange office.	**Je cherche un bureau de change.** [ʒə ʃɛrʃ œ̃ byro də ʃɑ̃:ʒ]
I'd like to change …	**Je voudrais changer …** [ʒə vudrɛ ʃɑ̃ʒe …]
What is the exchange rate?	**Quel est le taux de change?** [kɛl ɛ lə to də ʃɑ̃:ʒ?]
Do you need my passport?	**Avez-vous besoin de mon passeport?** [ave vu bəzwɛ̃ də mɔ̃ paspɔːr?]

Time

What time is it?	**Quelle heure est-il?** [kɛl œr ɛ-til?]
When?	**Quand?** [kɑ̃?]
At what time?	**À quelle heure?** [a kɛl œ:r?]
now | later | after …	**maintenant | plus tard | après …** [mɛ̃tnɑ̃ | ply tar | aprɛ …]

one o'clock	**une heure** [yn œ:r]
one fifteen	**une heure et quart** [yn œ:r e kar]
one thirty	**une heure et demie** [yn œ:r e dəmi]
one forty-five	**deux heures moins quart** [døzœr mwɛ̃ kar]

one | two | three	**un | deux | trois** [œ̃ | dø | trwɑ]
four | five | six	**quatre | cinq | six** [katr | sɛ̃k | sis]
seven | eight | nine	**sept | huit | neuf** [sɛt | ɥit | nœf]
ten | eleven | twelve	**dix | onze | douze** [dis | ɔ̃z | duz]

in …	**dans …** [dɑ̃ …]
five minutes	**cinq minutes** [sɛ̃k minyt]
ten minutes	**dix minutes** [di minyt]
fifteen minutes	**quinze minutes** [kɛ̃z minyt]
twenty minutes	**vingt minutes** [vɛ̃ minyt]

half an hour	**une demi-heure** [yn dəmiœr]
an hour	**une heure** [yn œ:r]

in the morning	**dans la matinée** [dɑ̃ la matine]
early in the morning	**tôt le matin** [to lə matɛ̃]
this morning	**ce matin** [sə matɛ̃]
tomorrow morning	**demain matin** [dəmɛ̃ matɛ̃]

at noon	**à midi** [a midi]
in the afternoon	**dans l'après-midi** [dɑ̃ laprɛmidi]
in the evening	**dans la soirée** [dɑ̃ la sware]
tonight	**ce soir** [sə swar]

at night	**la nuit** [la nɥi]
yesterday	**hier** [jɛr]
today	**aujourd'hui** [oʒurdɥi]
tomorrow	**demain** [dəmɛ̃]
the day after tomorrow	**après-demain** [aprɛdmɛ̃]

What day is it today?	**Quel jour sommes-nous aujourd'hui?** [kɛl ʒur sɔm-nu oʒurdɥi?]
It's ...	**Nous sommes ...** [nu sɔm ...]
Monday	**lundi** [lœ̃di]
Tuesday	**mardi** [mardi]
Wednesday	**mercredi** [mɛrkrədi]

Thursday	**jeudi** [ʒødi]
Friday	**vendredi** [vɑ̃drədi]
Saturday	**samedi** [samdi]
Sunday	**dimanche** [dimɑ̃ʃ]

Greetings. Introductions

Hello.
Bonjour.
[bõʒuːr]

Pleased to meet you.
Enchanté /Enchantée/
[ãʃãte]

Me too.
Moi aussi.
[mwa osi]

I'd like you to meet ...
Je voudrais vous présenter ...
[ʒə vudrɛ vu prezãte ...]

Nice to meet you.
Ravi /Ravie/ de vous rencontrer.
[ravi də vu rãkõtre.]

How are you?
Comment allez-vous?
[kɔmãtalevu?]

My name is ...
Je m'appelle ...
[ʒə mapɛl ...]

His name is ...
Il s'appelle ...
[il sapɛl ...]

Her name is ...
Elle s'appelle ...
[ɛl sapɛl ...]

What's your name?
Comment vous appelez-vous?
[kɔmã vuzaple-vu?]

What's his name?
Quel est son nom?
[kɛl ɛ sõ nõ?]

What's her name?
Quel est son nom?
[kɛl ɛ sõ nõ?]

What's your last name?
Quel est votre nom de famille?
[kɛl ɛ vɔtr nõ də famij?]

You can call me ...
Vous pouvez m'appeler ...
[vu puve maple ...]

Where are you from?
D'où êtes-vous?
[du ɛt-vu?]

I'm from ...
Je suis de ...
[ʒə sɥi də ...]

What do you do for a living?
Qu'est-ce que vous faites dans la vie?
[kɛs kə vu fɛt dã la vi?]

Who is this?
Qui est-ce?
[ki ɛs?]

Who is he?
Qui est-il?
[ki ɛ-til?]

Who is she?
Qui est-elle?
[ki ɛtɛl?]

Who are they?
Qui sont-ils?
[ki sõ til?]

This is ...	**C'est ...** [sɛ ...]
my friend (masc.)	**mon ami** [mɔn ami]
my friend (fem.)	**mon amie** [mɔn ami]
my husband	**mon mari** [mɔ̃ mari]
my wife	**ma femme** [ma fam]
my father	**mon père** [mɔ̃ pɛr]
my mother	**ma mère** [ma mɛr]
my brother	**mon frère** [mɔ̃ frɛr]
my sister	**ma soeur** [ma sœr]
my son	**mon fils** [mɔ̃ fis]
my daughter	**ma fille** [ma fij]
This is our son.	**C'est notre fils.** [sɛ nɔtr fis]
This is our daughter.	**C'est notre fille.** [sɛ nɔtr fij]
These are my children.	**Ce sont mes enfants.** [sə sɔ̃ mezɑ̃fɑ̃]
These are our children.	**Ce sont nos enfants.** [sə sɔ̃ nozɑ̃fɑ̃]

Farewells

Good bye!	**Au revoir!** [o rəvwa:r!]
Bye! (inform.)	**Salut!** [saly!]
See you tomorrow.	**À demain.** [a dəmɛ̃]
See you soon.	**À bientôt.** [a bjɛ̃to]
See you at seven.	**On se revoit à sept heures.** [ɔ̃ sə rəvwa a sɛt œ:r]

Have fun!	**Amusez-vous bien!** [amyze vu bjɛ̃!]
Talk to you later.	**On se voit plus tard.** [ɔ̃ sə vwa ply ta:r]
Have a nice weekend.	**Bonne fin de semaine.** [bɔn fɛ̃ də səmɛn]
Good night.	**Bonne nuit.** [bɔn nɥi]

It's time for me to go.	**Il est l'heure que je parte.** [il ɛ lœr kə ʒə part]
I have to go.	**Je dois m'en aller.** [ʒə dwa mãnale]
I will be right back.	**Je reviens tout de suite.** [ʒə rəvjɛ̃ tu də sɥit]

It's late.	**Il est tard.** [il ɛ ta:r]
I have to get up early.	**Je dois me lever tôt.** [ʒə dwa mə ləve to]
I'm leaving tomorrow.	**Je pars demain.** [ʒə par dəmɛ̃]
We're leaving tomorrow.	**Nous partons demain.** [nu partɔ̃ dəmɛ̃]

Have a nice trip!	**Bon voyage!** [bɔ̃ vwaja:ʒ!]
It was nice meeting you.	**Enchanté de faire votre connaissance.** [ãʃãte də fɛr vɔtr kɔnɛsã:s]
It was nice talking to you.	**Heureux /Heureuse/ d'avoir parlé avec vous.** [ørø /ørøz/ davwar parle avɛk vu]

Thanks for everything.	**Merci pour tout.**
	[mɛrsi pur tu]
I had a very good time.	**Je me suis vraiment amusé /amusée/**
	[ʒə mə sʉi vrɛmɑ̃ amyze]
We had a very good time.	**Nous nous sommes vraiment amusés**
	/amusées/
	[nu nu sɔm vrɛmɑ̃ amyze]
It was really great.	**C'était vraiment plaisant.**
	[setɛ vrɛmɑ̃ plɛzɑ̃]
I'm going to miss you.	**Vous allez me manquer.**
	[vuzale mə mɑ̃ke]
We're going to miss you.	**Vous allez nous manquer.**
	[vuzale nu mɑ̃ke]
Good luck!	**Bonne chance!**
	[bɔn ʃɑ̃:s!]
Say hi to …	**Mes salutations à …**
	[me salytasjɔ̃ a …]

Foreign language

I don't understand.	**Je ne comprends pas.** [ʒə nə kɔ̃prɑ̃ pɑ]
Write it down, please.	**Écrivez-le, s'il vous plaît.** [ekrive lə, sil vu plɛ]
Do you speak ...?	**Parlez-vous ...?** [parle vu ...?]

I speak a little bit of ...	**Je parle un peu ...** [ʒə parl œ̃ pø ...]
English	**anglais** [ɑ̃glɛ]
Turkish	**turc** [tyrk]
Arabic	**arabe** [arab]
French	**français** [frɑ̃sɛ]

German	**allemand** [almɑ̃]
Italian	**italien** [italjɛ̃]
Spanish	**espagnol** [ɛspaɲɔl]
Portuguese	**portugais** [pɔrtygɛ]
Chinese	**chinois** [ʃinwa]
Japanese	**japonais** [ʒapɔnɛ]

Can you repeat that, please.	**Pouvez-vous le répéter, s'il vous plaît.** [puve vu lə repete, sil vu plɛ]
I understand.	**Je comprends.** [ʒə kɔ̃prɑ̃]
I don't understand.	**Je ne comprends pas.** [ʒə nə kɔ̃prɑ̃ pɑ]
Please speak more slowly.	**Parlez plus lentement, s'il vous plaît.** [parle ply lɑ̃tmɑ̃, sil vu plɛ]

Is that correct? (Am I saying it right?)	**Est-ce que c'est correct?** [ɛskə sɛ kɔrrɛkt?]
What is this? (What does this mean?)	**Qu'est-ce que c'est?** [kɛskə sɛ?]

Apologies

Excuse me, please.	**Excusez-moi, s'il vous plaît.**
	[ɛkskyze mwa, sil vu plɛ]
I'm sorry.	**Je suis désolé /désolée/**
	[ʒə sɥi dezɔle]
I'm really sorry.	**Je suis vraiment /désolée/**
	[ʒə sɥi vrɛmɑ̃ dezɔle]
Sorry, it's my fault.	**Désolé /Désolée/, c'est ma faute.**
	[dezɔle, sɛ ma fot]
My mistake.	**Au temps pour moi.**
	[otɑ̃ pur mwa]

May I …?	**Puis-je … ?**
	[pɥiʒ …?]
Do you mind if I …?	**Ça vous dérange si je …?**
	[sa vu derɑ̃ʒ si ʒə …?]
It's OK.	**Ce n'est pas grave.**
	[sə nɛ pɑ graːv]
It's all right.	**Ça va.**
	[sa va]
Don't worry about it.	**Ne vous inquiétez pas.**
	[nə vuzɛ̃kjete pɑ]

Agreement

Yes.	**Oui** [wi]
Yes, sure.	**Oui, bien sûr.** [wi, bjɛ̃ sy:r]
OK (Good!)	**Bien.** [bjɛ̃]
Very well.	**Très bien.** [trɛ bjɛ̃]
Certainly!	**Bien sûr!** [bjɛ̃sy:r!]
I agree.	**Je suis d'accord.** [ʒə sɥi dakɔ:r]

That's correct.	**C'est correct.** [sɛ kɔrrɛkt]
That's right.	**C'est exact.** [sɛtɛgzakt]
You're right.	**Vous avez raison.** [vuzave rɛzɔ̃]
I don't mind.	**Je ne suis pas contre.** [ʒə nə sɥi pɑ kɔ̃tr]
Absolutely right.	**Tout à fait correct.** [tutafɛ kɔrrɛkt]

It's possible.	**C'est possible.** [sɛ pɔsibl]
That's a good idea.	**C'est une bonne idée.** [sɛtyn bɔn ide]
I can't say no.	**Je ne peux pas dire non.** [ʒə nə pø pɑ dir nɔ̃]
I'd be happy to.	**J'en serai ravi /ravie/** [ʒɑ̃ səre ravi:]
With pleasure.	**Avec plaisir.** [avɛk plezi:r]

Refusal. Expressing doubt

No.	**Non** [nɔ̃]
Certainly not.	**Absolument pas.** [absɔlymɑ̃ pɑ]

I don't agree.	**Je ne suis pas d'accord.** [ʒə nə sɥi pɑ dakɔ:r]
I don't think so.	**Je ne le crois pas.** [ʒə nə lə krwa pɑ]
It's not true.	**Ce n'est pas vrai.** [sə nɛ pɑ vrɛ]

You are wrong.	**Vous avez tort.** [vuzave tɔ:r]
I think you are wrong.	**Je pense que vous avez tort.** [ʒə pɑ̃s kə vuzave tɔ:r]

I'm not sure.	**Je ne suis pas sûr /sûre/** [ʒə nə sɥi pɑ sy:r]
It's impossible.	**C'est impossible.** [sɛtɛ̃pɔsibl]
Nothing of the kind (sort)!	**Pas du tout!** [pɑ dy tu!]

The exact opposite.	**Au contraire!** [o kɔ̃trɛ:r!]
I'm against it.	**Je suis contre.** [ʒə sɥi kɔ̃tr]
I don't care.	**Ça m'est égal.** [sa mɛ tegal]
I have no idea.	**Je n'ai aucune idée.** [ʒə ne okyn ide]
I doubt that.	**Je doute que cela soit ainsi.** [ʒə dut kə səla swa ɛ̃si]

Sorry, I can't.	**Désolé /Désolée/, je ne peux pas.** [dezɔle, ʒə nə pø pɑ]
Sorry, I don't want to.	**Désolé /Désolée/, je ne veux pas.** [dezɔle, ʒə nə vø pɑ]

Thank you, but I don't need this.	**Merci, mais ça ne m'intéresse pas.** [mɛrsi, mɛ sa nə mɛ̃terɛs pɑ]
It's late.	**Il se fait tard.** [il sə fɛ ta:r]

I have to get up early.

Je dois me lever tôt.
[ʒə dwa mə ləve to]

I don't feel well.

Je ne me sens pas bien.
[ʒə nə mə sã pa bjɛ̃]

Expressing gratitude

Thank you.
Merci.
[mɛrsi]

Thank you very much.
Merci beaucoup.
[mɛrsi boku]

I really appreciate it.
Je l'apprécie beaucoup.
[ʒə lapresi boku]

I'm really grateful to you.
Je vous suis très reconnaissant.
[ʒə vu sɥi trɛ rəkɔnɛsã]

We are really grateful to you.
**Nous vous sommes
très reconnaissant.**
[nu vu sɔm
trɛ rəkɔnɛsã]

Thank you for your time.
Merci pour votre temps.
[mɛrsi pur vɔtr tã]

Thanks for everything.
Merci pour tout.
[mɛrsi pur tu]

Thank you for ...
Merci pour ...
[mɛrsi pur ...]

your help
votre aide
[vɔtr ɛd]

a nice time
les bons moments passés
[le bõ mɔmã pase]

a wonderful meal
un repas merveilleux
[œ̃ rəpa mɛrvɛjø]

a pleasant evening
cette agréable soirée
[sɛt agreabl sware]

a wonderful day
cette merveilleuse journée
[sɛt mɛrvɛjøz ʒurne]

an amazing journey
une excursion extraordinaire
[yn ɛkskyrsjõ ɛkstraɔrdinɛr]

Don't mention it.
Il n'y a pas de quoi.
[il njapɑ də kwa]

You are welcome.
Je vous en prie.
[ʒə vuzãpri]

Any time.
Mon plaisir.
[mõ plezi:r]

My pleasure.
**J'ai été heureux /heureuse/
de vous aider.**
[ʒe ete ørø /ørøz/
də vuzɛde]

Forget it. It's alright.

Ça va. N'y pensez plus.
[sa va. ni pɑ̃se ply]

Don't worry about it.

Ne vous inquiétez pas.
[nə vuzɛ̃kjete pɑ]

Congratulations. Best wishes

Congratulations!

Félicitations!
[felisitasjɔ̃!]

Happy birthday!

Joyeux anniversaire!
[ʒwajø zanivɛrsɛːr!]

Merry Christmas!

Joyeux Noël!
[ʒwajø nɔɛl!]

Happy New Year!

Bonne Année!
[bɔn ane!]

Happy Easter!

Joyeuses Pâques!
[ʒwajøz pɑk!]

Happy Hanukkah!

Joyeux Hanoukka!
[ʒwajø anuka!]

I'd like to propose a toast.

Je voudrais proposer un toast.
[ʒə vudrɛ prɔpoze œ̃ tost]

Cheers!

Santé!
[sɑ̃te!]

Let's drink to ...!

Buvons à ...!
[byvɔ̃ a ...!]

To our success!

À notre succès!
[a nɔtr syksɛ!]

To your success!

À votre succès!
[a vɔtr syksɛ!]

Good luck!

Bonne chance!
[bɔn ʃɑ̃ːs!]

Have a nice day!

Bonne journée!
[bɔn ʒurne!]

Have a good holiday!

Passez de bonnes vacances !
[pɑse də bɔn vakɑ̃s!]

Have a safe journey!

Bon voyage!
[bɔ̃ vwajaːʒ!]

I hope you get better soon!

Rétablissez-vous vite.
[retablise-vu vit]

Socializing

Why are you sad?	**Pourquoi êtes-vous si triste?** [purkwa ɛt-vu si trist?]
Smile! Cheer up!	**Souriez!** [surje!]
Are you free tonight?	**Êtes-vous libre ce soir?** [ɛt-vu libr sə swa:r?]

May I offer you a drink?	**Puis-je vous offrir un verre?** [pɥiʒ vu zɔfrir œ̃ vɛ:r?]
Would you like to dance?	**Voulez-vous danser?** [vule-vu dɑ̃se?]
Let's go to the movies.	**Et si on va au cinéma?** [e si ɔ̃va o sinema?]

May I invite you to ...?	**Puis-je vous inviter ...?** [pɥiʒ vu zɛ̃vite ...?]
a restaurant	**au restaurant** [o rɛstɔrɑ̃]
the movies	**au cinéma** [o sinema]
the theater	**au théâtre** [o teatr]
go for a walk	**pour une promenade** [pur yn prɔmnad]

At what time?	**À quelle heure?** [a kɛl œ:r?]
tonight	**ce soir** [sə swar]
at six	**à six heures** [a siz œ:r]
at seven	**à sept heures** [a sɛt œ:r]
at eight	**à huit heures** [a ɥit œ:r]
at nine	**à neuf heures** [a nœv œ:r]

Do you like it here?	**Est-ce que vous aimez cet endroit?** [ɛskə vuzɛme sɛt ɑ̃drwa?]
Are you here with someone?	**Êtes-vous ici avec quelqu'un?** [ɛt-vu isi avɛk kelkœ̃?]
I'm with my friend.	**Je suis avec mon ami.** [ʒə sɥi avɛk mɔn ami]

I'm with my friends.	**Je suis avec mes amis.** [ʒə sɥi avɛk mezami]
No, I'm alone.	**Non, je suis seul /seule/** [nõ, ʒə sɥi sœl]

Do you have a boyfriend?	**As-tu un copain?** [a ty œ̃ kɔpɛ̃?]
I have a boyfriend.	**J'ai un copain.** [ʒe œ̃ kɔpɛ̃]
Do you have a girlfriend?	**As-tu une copine?** [a ty yn kɔpin?]
I have a girlfriend.	**J'ai une copine.** [ʒe yn kɔpin]

Can I see you again?	**Est-ce que je peux te revoir?** [ɛskə ʒə pø tə rəvwa:r?]
Can I call you?	**Est-ce que je peux t'appeler?** [ɛskə ʒə pø taple?]
Call me. (Give me a call.)	**Appelle-moi.** [apɛl mwa]
What's your number?	**Quel est ton numéro?** [kɛl ɛ tõ nymero?]
I miss you.	**Tu me manques.** [ty mə mɑ̃:k]

You have a beautiful name.	**Vous avez un très beau nom.** [vuzave œ̃ trɛ bo nõ]
I love you.	**Je t'aime.** [ʒə tɛm]
Will you marry me?	**Veux-tu te marier avec moi?** [vø-ty tə marje avɛk mwa?]
You're kidding!	**Vous plaisantez!** [vu plɛzɑ̃te!]
I'm just kidding.	**Je plaisante.** [ʒə plɛzɑ̃:t]

Are you serious?	**Êtes-vous sérieux /sérieuse/?** [ɛt-vu serjø /serjøz/?]
I'm serious.	**Je suis sérieux /sérieuse/** [ʒə sɥi serjø /serjøz/]
Really?!	**Vraiment?!** [vrɛmɑ̃?!]
It's unbelievable!	**C'est incroyable!** [sɛtɛ̃krwajabl!]
I don't believe you.	**Je ne vous crois pas.** [ʒə nə vu krwa pɑ]
I can't.	**Je ne peux pas.** [ʒə nə pø pɑ]
I don't know.	**Je ne sais pas.** [ʒə nə sɛ pɑ]
I don't understand you.	**Je ne vous comprends pas** [ʒə nə vu kõprɑ̃ pɑ]

Please go away.   **Laissez-moi! Allez-vous-en!**
                                   [lɛse-mwa! ale-vuzɑ̃!]

Leave me alone!   **Laissez-moi tranquille!**
                                   [lɛse-mwa trɑ̃kil!]

I can't stand him.   **Je ne le supporte pas.**
                                   [ʒə nə lə sypɔrt pɑ]

You are disgusting!   **Vous êtes dégoûtant!**
                                   [vuzɛt degutɑ̃!]

I'll call the police!   **Je vais appeler la police!**
                                   [ʒə ve aple la pɔlis!]

Sharing impressions. Emotions

I like it.	**J'aime ça.** [ʒɛm sa]
Very nice.	**C'est gentil.** [sɛ ʒɑ̃ti]
That's great!	**C'est super!** [sɛ sypɛr!]
It's not bad.	**C'est assez bien.** [sɛtase bjɛ̃]

I don't like it.	**Je n'aime pas ça.** [ʒə nɛm pɑ sa]
It's not good.	**Ce n'est pas bien.** [sə nɛ pɑ bjɛ̃]
It's bad.	**C'est mauvais.** [sɛ mɔvɛ]
It's very bad.	**Ce n'est pas bien du tout.** [sə nɛ pɑ bjɛ̃ dy tu]
It's disgusting.	**C'est dégoûtant.** [sɛ degutɑ̃]

I'm happy.	**Je suis content /contente/** [ʒə sɥi kɔ̃tɑ̃ /kɔ̃tɑ̃t/]
I'm content.	**Je suis heureux /heureuse/** [ʒə sɥi ørø /ørøz/]
I'm in love.	**Je suis amoureux /amoureuse/** [ʒə sɥi amurø /amurøz/]
I'm calm.	**Je suis calme.** [ʒə sɥi kalm]
I'm bored.	**Je m'ennuie.** [ʒə mɑ̃nɥi]

I'm tired.	**Je suis fatigué /fatiguée/** [ʒə sɥi fatige]
I'm sad.	**Je suis triste.** [ʒə sɥi trist]
I'm frightened.	**J'ai peur.** [ʒe pœːr]

I'm angry.	**Je suis fâché /fâchée/** [ʒə sɥi faʃe]
I'm worried.	**Je suis inquiet /inquiète/** [ʒə sɥi ɛ̃kjɛ /ɛ̃kjɛt/]
I'm nervous.	**Je suis nerveux /nerveuse/** [ʒə sɥi nɛrvø /nɛrvøz/]

I'm jealous. (envious)

Je suis jaloux /jalouse/
[ʒə sɥi ʒalu /ʒaluz/]

I'm surprised.

Je suis surpris /surprise/
[ʒə sɥi syrpri /syrpriz/]

I'm perplexed.

Je suis gêné /gênée/
[ʒə sɥi ʒɛne]

Problems. Accidents

I've got a problem.

J'ai un problème.
[ʒe œ̃ prɔblɛm]

We've got a problem.

Nous avons un problème.
[nuzavɔ̃ œ̃ prɔblɛm]

I'm lost.

Je suis perdu /perdue/
[ʒə sɥi pɛrdy]

I missed the last bus (train).

J'ai manqué le dernier bus (train).
[ʒe mãke lə dɛrnje bys (trɛ̃)]

I don't have any money left.

Je n'ai plus d'argent.
[ʒə ne ply darʒã]

I've lost my ...

J'ai perdu mon ...
[ʒe pɛrdy mɔ̃ ...]

Someone stole my ...

On m'a volé mon ...
[ɔ̃ ma vɔle mɔ̃ ...]

passport

passeport
[paspɔːr]

wallet

portefeuille
[pɔrtəfœj]

papers

papiers
[papje]

ticket

billet
[bijɛ]

money

argent
[arʒã]

handbag

sac à main
[sak a mɛ̃]

camera

appareil photo
[aparɛj fɔto]

laptop

portable
[pɔrtabl]

tablet computer

ma tablette
[ma tablɛt]

mobile phone

mobile
[mɔbil]

Help me!

Au secours!
[o səkuːr!]

What's happened?

Qu'est-il arrivé?
[kɛtil arive?]

fire

un incendie
[œn ɛ̃sãdi]

shooting	**des coups de feu** [de ku də fø]
murder	**un meurtre** [œ̃ mœrtr]
explosion	**une explosion** [yn ɛksplozjɔ̃]
fight	**une bagarre** [yn bagar]

Call the police!	**Appelez la police!** [aple la polis!]
Please hurry up!	**Dépêchez-vous, s'il vous plaît!** [depɛʃe-vu, sil vu plɛ!]
I'm looking for the police station.	**Je cherche le commissariat de police.** [ʒə ʃerʃ lə komisarja də polis]
I need to make a call.	**Il me faut faire un appel.** [il mə fo fɛr œn apɛl]
May I use your phone?	**Puis-je utiliser votre téléphone?** [pɥiʒ ytilize votr telefon?]

I've been …	**J'ai été …** [ʒe ete …]
mugged	**agressé /agressée/** [agrɛse]
robbed	**volé /volée/** [vole]
raped	**violée** [vjole]
attacked (beaten up)	**attaqué /attaquée/** [atake]

Are you all right?	**Est-ce que ça va?** [ɛskə sa va?]
Did you see who it was?	**Avez-vous vu qui c'était?** [ave vu vy ki setɛ?]
Would you be able to recognize the person?	**Pourriez-vous reconnaître cette personne?** [purje-vu rəkonɛtr sɛt persɔn?]
Are you sure?	**Vous êtes sûr?** [vuzɛt sy:r?]

Please calm down.	**Calmez-vous, s'il vous plaît.** [kalme-vu, sil vu plɛ]
Take it easy!	**Calmez-vous!** [kalme-vu!]
Don't worry!	**Ne vous inquiétez pas.** [nə vuzɛ̃kjete pɑ]
Everything will be fine.	**Tout ira bien.** [tutira bjɛ̃]
Everything's all right.	**Ça va. Tout va bien.** [sa va. tu va bjɛ̃]

Come here, please.

I have some questions for you.

Wait a moment, please.

Do you have any I.D.?

Thanks. You can leave now.

Hands behind your head!

You're under arrest!

Venez ici, s'il vous plaît.
[vəne isi, sil vu plɛ]

J'ai des questions à vous poser.
[ʒe de kɛstjɔ̃ a vu poze]

Attendez un moment, s'il vous plaît.
[atɑ̃de œ̃ mɔmɑ̃, sil vu plɛ]

Avez-vous une carte d'identité?
[ave vu yn kart didɑ̃tite?]

Merci. Vous pouvez partir maintenant.
[mɛrsi. vu puve partir mɛ̃tnɑ̃]

Les mains derrière la tête!
[le mɛ̃ dɛrjɛr la tɛt!]

Vous êtes arrêté!
[vuzɛt arɛte!]

Health problems

Please help me.	**Aidez-moi, s'il vous plaît.** [ɛde-mwa, sil vu plɛ]
I don't feel well.	**Je ne me sens pas bien.** [ʒə nə mə sã pɑ bjɛ̃]
My husband doesn't feel well.	**Mon mari ne se sent pas bien.** [mɔ̃ mari nə sə sã pɑ bjɛ̃]
My son ...	**Mon fils ...** [mɔ̃ fis ...]
My father ...	**Mon père ...** [mɔ̃ pɛr ...]

My wife doesn't feel well.	**Ma femme ne se sent pas bien.** [ma fam nə sə sã pɑ bjɛ̃]
My daughter ...	**Ma fille ...** [ma fij ...]
My mother ...	**Ma mère ...** [ma mɛr ...]

I've got a ...	**J'ai mal ...** [ʒe mal ...]
headache	**à la tête** [a la tɛt]
sore throat	**à la gorge** [a la gɔrʒ]
stomach ache	**à l'estomac** [a lɛstɔma]
toothache	**aux dents** [o dã]

I feel dizzy.	**J'ai le vertige.** [ʒe lə vɛrti:ʒ]
He has a fever.	**Il a de la fièvre.** [il a də la fjɛ:vr]
She has a fever.	**Elle a de la fièvre.** [ɛl a də la fjɛ:vr]
I can't breathe.	**Je ne peux pas respirer.** [ʒə nə pø pɑ rɛspire]

I'm short of breath.	**J'ai du mal à respirer.** [ʒe dy mal a rɛspire]
I am asthmatic.	**Je suis asthmatique.** [ʒə sɥi asmatik]
I am diabetic.	**Je suis diabétique.** [ʒə sɥi djabetik]

I can't sleep.	**Je ne peux pas dormir.**
	[ʒə nə pø pɑ dɔrmi:r]
food poisoning	**intoxication alimentaire**
	[ɛ̃tɔksikasjɔ̃ alimɑ̃tɛr]

It hurts here.	**Ça fait mal ici.**
	[sa fɛ mal isi]
Help me!	**Aidez-moi!**
	[ɛde-mwa!]
I am here!	**Je suis ici!**
	[ʒə sɥi isi!]
We are here!	**Nous sommes ici!**
	[nu sɔm isi!]
Get me out of here!	**Sortez-moi d'ici!**
	[sɔrte mwa disi!]
I need a doctor.	**J'ai besoin d'un docteur.**
	[ʒe bəzwɛ̃ dœ̃ dɔktœ:r]
I can't move.	**Je ne peux pas bouger!**
	[ʒə nə pø pɑ buʒe!]
I can't move my legs.	**Je ne peux pas bouger mes jambes.**
	[ʒə nə pø pɑ buʒe me ʒɑ̃:b]

I have a wound.	**Je suis blessé /blessée/**
	[ʒə sɥi blɛse]
Is it serious?	**Est-ce que c'est sérieux?**
	[ɛskə sɛ serjø?]
My documents are in my pocket.	**Mes papiers sont dans ma poche.**
	[me papje sɔ̃ dɑ̃ ma pɔʃ]
Calm down!	**Calmez-vous!**
	[kalme vu!]
May I use your phone?	**Puis-je utiliser votre téléphone?**
	[pɥiʒ ytilize vɔtr telefɔn?]

Call an ambulance!	**Appelez une ambulance!**
	[aple yn ɑ̃bylɑ̃:s!]
It's urgent!	**C'est urgent!**
	[sɛtyrʒɑ̃!]
It's an emergency!	**C'est une urgence!**
	[sɛtyn yrʒɑ̃:s!]
Please hurry up!	**Dépêchez-vous, s'il vous plaît!**
	[depɛʃe-vu, sil vu plɛ!]
Would you please call a doctor?	**Appelez le docteur, s'il vous plaît.**
	[aple lə dɔktœ:r, sil vu plɛ]
Where is the hospital?	**Où est l'hôpital?**
	[u ɛ lɔpital?]

How are you feeling?	**Comment vous sentez-vous?**
	[kɔmɑ̃ vu sɑ̃te-vu?]
Are you all right?	**Est-ce que ça va?**
	[ɛskə sa va?]
What's happened?	**Qu'est-il arrivé?**
	[kɛtil arive?]

I feel better now.

Je me sens mieux maintenant.
[ʒə mə sɑ̃ mjø mɛ̃tnɑ̃]

It's OK.

Ça va. Tout va bien.
[sa va. tu va bjɛ̃]

It's all right.

Ça va.
[sa va]

At the pharmacy

pharmacy (drugstore)
pharmacie
[farmasi]

24-hour pharmacy
pharmacie 24 heures
[farmasi vɛ̃katr œr]

Where is the closest pharmacy?
**Où se trouve la pharmacie
la plus proche?**
[u sə truv la farmasi
la ply prɔʃ?]

Is it open now?
Est-elle ouverte en ce moment?
[ɛtɛl uvɛrt ɑ̃ sə mɔmɑ̃?]

At what time does it open?
À quelle heure ouvre-t-elle?
[a kɛl œr uvr tɛl?]

At what time does it close?
à quelle heure ferme-t-elle?
[a kɛl œr fɛrm tɛl?]

Is it far?
C'est loin?
[sɛ lwɛ̃?]

Can I get there on foot?
Est-ce que je peux y aller à pied?
[ɛskə ʒə pø i ale a pje?]

Can you show me on the map?
**Pouvez-vous me le montrer
sur la carte?**
[puve vu mə lə mɔ̃tre
syr la kart?]

Please give me something for ...
**Pouvez-vous me donner
quelque chose contre ...**
[puve vu mə dɔne
kɛlkə ʃoz kɔ̃tr ...]

a headache
le mal de tête
[lə mal də tɛt]

a cough
la toux
[la tu]

a cold
le rhume
[lə rym]

the flu
la grippe
[la grip]

a fever
la fièvre
[la fjɛ:vr]

a stomach ache
un mal d'estomac
[œ̃ mal dɛstɔma]

nausea
la nausée
[la noze]

diarrhea	**la diarrhée** [la djare]
constipation	**la constipation** [la kõstipasjõ]
pain in the back	**un mal de dos** [œ̃ mal də do]
chest pain	**les douleurs de poitrine** [le dulœr də pwatrin]
side stitch	**les points de côté** [le pwɛ̃ də kote]
abdominal pain	**les douleurs abdominales** [le dulœr abdɔminal]
pill	**une pilule** [yn pilyl]
ointment, cream	**un onguent, une crème** [œn õgã, yn krɛm]
syrup	**un sirop** [œ̃ siro]
spray	**un spray** [œ̃ sprɛ]
drops	**les gouttes** [le gut]
You need to go to the hospital.	**Vous devez allez à l'hôpital.** [vu dəve ale a lɔpital]
health insurance	**assurance maladie** [asyrãs maladi]
prescription	**prescription** [prɛskripsjõ]
insect repellant	**produit anti-insecte** [prɔdɥi ãti-ɛ̃sɛkt]
Band Aid	**bandages adhésifs** [bãdaʒ adezif]

The bare minimum

Excuse me, ...	**Excusez-moi, ...** [ɛkskyzə mwa, ...]
Hello.	**Bonjour** [bɔ̃ʒuːr]
Thank you.	**Merci** [mɛrsi]
Good bye.	**Au revoir** [o rəvwaːr]
Yes.	**Oui** [wi]
No.	**Non** [nɔ̃]
I don't know.	**Je ne sais pas.** [ʒə nə sɛ pɑ]
Where? | Where to? | When?	**Où? | Où? | Quand?** [u? | u? | kɑ̃?]

I need ...	**J'ai besoin de ...** [ʒe bəzwɛ̃ də ...]
I want ...	**Je veux ...** [ʒə vø ...]
Do you have ...?	**Avez-vous ... ?** [ave vu ...?]
Is there a ... here?	**Est-ce qu'il y a ... ici?** [ɛs kilja ... isi?]
May I ...?	**Puis-je ... ?** [pɥiʒ ...?]
..., please (polite request)	**..., s'il vous plaît** [..., sil vu plɛ]

I'm looking for ...	**Je cherche ...** [ʒə ʃɛrʃ ...]
restroom	**les toilettes** [le twalɛt]
ATM	**un distributeur** [œ̃ distribytœːr]
pharmacy (drugstore)	**une pharmacie** [yn farmasi]
hospital	**l'hôpital** [lopital]
police station	**le commissariat de police** [lə kɔmisarja də pɔlis]
subway	**une station de métro** [yn stasjɔ̃ də metro]

taxi	**un taxi** [œ̃ taksi]
train station	**la gare** [la gar]

My name is …	**Je m'appelle …** [ʒə mapɛl …]
What's your name?	**Comment vous appelez-vous?** [kɔmɑ̃ vuzaple-vu?]
Could you please help me?	**Aidez-moi, s'il vous plaît.** [ɛde-mwa, sil vu plɛ]
I've got a problem.	**J'ai un problème.** [ʒe œ̃ prɔblɛm]
I don't feel well.	**Je ne me sens pas bien.** [ʒə nə mə sɑ̃ pɑ bjɛ̃]
Call an ambulance!	**Appelez une ambulance!** [aple yn ɑ̃bylɑ̃:s!]
May I make a call?	**Puis-je faire un appel?** [pɥiʒ fɛr œn apɛl?]

I'm sorry.	**Excusez-moi.** [ɛkskyze mwa]
You're welcome.	**Je vous en prie.** [ʒə vuzɑ̃pri]

I, me	**je, moi** [ʒə, mwa]
you (inform.)	**tu, toi** [ty, twa]
he	**il** [il]
she	**elle** [ɛl]
they (masc.)	**ils** [il]
they (fem.)	**elles** [ɛl]
we	**nous** [nu]
you (pl)	**vous** [vu]
you (sg, form.)	**Vous** [vu]

ENTRANCE	**ENTRÉE** [ɑ̃tre]
EXIT	**SORTIE** [sɔrti]
OUT OF ORDER	**HORS SERVICE | EN PANNE** [ɔr sɛrvis | ɑ̃ pan]
CLOSED	**FERMÉ** [fɛrme]

OPEN

OUVERT
[uvɛr]

FOR WOMEN

POUR LES FEMMES
[pur le fam]

FOR MEN

POUR LES HOMMES
[pur le zɔm]

TOPICAL VOCABULARY

This section contains more than 3,000 of the most important words.
The dictionary will provide invaluable assistance while traveling abroad, because frequently individual words are enough for you to be understood.
The dictionary includes a convenient transcription of each foreign word

T&P Books Publishing

VOCABULARY
CONTENTS

T&P Books Publishing

T&P BOOKS

BASIC CONCEPTS

T&P Books Publishing

1. Pronouns

I, me	**je**	[ʒə]
you	**tu**	[ty]
he	**il**	[il]
she	**elle**	[ɛl]
it	**ça**	[sa]
we	**nous**	[nu]
you (to a group)	**vous**	[vu]
they (masc.)	**ils**	[il]
they (fem.)	**elles**	[ɛl]

2. Greetings. Salutations

Hello! (fam.)	**Bonjour!**	[bɔ̃ʒur]
Hello! (form.)	**Bonjour!**	[bɔ̃ʒur]
Good morning!	**Bonjour!**	[bɔ̃ʒur]
Good afternoon!	**Bonjour!**	[bɔ̃ʒur]
Good evening!	**Bonsoir!**	[bɔ̃swar]
to say hello	**dire bonjour**	[dir bɔ̃ʒur]
Hi! (hello)	**Salut!**	[saly]
greeting (n)	**salut** (m)	[saly]
to greet (vt)	**saluer** (vt)	[salɥe]
How are you? (form.)	**Comment allez-vous?**	[kɔmɑ̃talevu]
How are you? (fam.)	**Comment ça va?**	[kɔmɑ̃ sa va]
What's new?	**Quoi de neuf?**	[kwa də nœf]
Bye-Bye! Goodbye!	**Au revoir!**	[orəvwar]
See you soon!	**À bientôt!**	[a bjɛ̃to]
Farewell!	**Adieu!**	[adjø]
to say goodbye	**dire au revoir**	[dir ərəvwar]
So long!	**Salut!**	[saly]
Thank you!	**Merci!**	[mɛrsi]
Thank you very much!	**Merci beaucoup!**	[mɛrsi boku]
You're welcome	**Je vous en prie**	[ʒə vuzɑ̃pri]
Don't mention it!	**Il n'y a pas de quoi**	[il njapɑ də kwa]
It was nothing	**Pas de quoi**	[pɑ də kwa]
Excuse me! (fam.)	**Excuse-moi!**	[ɛkskyz mwa]
Excuse me! (form.)	**Excusez-moi!**	[ɛkskyze mwa]

to excuse (forgive)	**excuser** (vt)	[ɛkskyze]
to apologize (vi)	**s'excuser** (vp)	[sɛkskyze]
My apologies	**Mes excuses**	[me zɛkskyz]
I'm sorry!	**Pardonnez-moi!**	[pardɔne mwa]
to forgive (vt)	**pardonner** (vt)	[pardɔne]
It's okay!	**C'est pas grave**	[sepagrav]
please (adv)	**s'il vous plaît**	[silvuple]
Don't forget!	**N'oubliez pas!**	[nublije pɑ]
Certainly!	**Bien sûr!**	[bjɛ̃ sy:r]
Of course not!	**Bien sûr que non!**	[bjɛ̃ syr kə nɔ̃]
Okay! (I agree)	**D'accord!**	[dakɔr]
That's enough!	**Ça suffit!**	[sa syfi]

3. Questions

Who?	**Qui?**	[ki]
What?	**Quoi?**	[kwa]
Where? (at, in)	**Où?**	[u]
Where (to)?	**Où?**	[u]
From where?	**D'où?**	[du]
When?	**Quand?**	[kɑ̃]
Why? (What for?)	**Pourquoi?**	[purkwa]
Why? (reason)	**Pourquoi?**	[purkwa]
What for?	**À quoi bon?**	[ɑ kwa bɔ̃]
How? (in what way)	**Comment?**	[kɔmɑ̃]
What? (What kind of ...?)	**Quel?**	[kɛl]
Which?	**Lequel?**	[ləkɛl]
To whom?	**À qui?**	[ɑ ki]
About whom?	**De qui?**	[də ki]
About what?	**De quoi?**	[də kwa]
With whom?	**Avec qui?**	[avɛk ki]
How many? How much?	**Combien?**	[kɔ̃bjɛ̃]
Whose?	**À qui?**	[ɑ ki]

4. Prepositions

with (accompanied by)	**avec ...** (prep)	[avɛk]
without	**sans ...** (prep)	[sɑ̃]
to (indicating direction)	**à ...** (prep)	[a]
about (talking ~ ...)	**de ...** (prep)	[də]
before (in time)	**avant** (prep)	[avɑ̃]
in front of ...	**devant ...** (prep)	[dəvɑ̃]
under (beneath, below)	**sous ...** (prep)	[su]
above (over)	**au-dessus de ...** (prep)	[odsy də]

on (atop)	**sur** ... (prep)	[syr]
from (off, out of)	**de** ... (prep)	[də]
of (made from)	**en** ... (prep)	[ã]
in (e.g., ~ ten minutes)	**dans** ... (prep)	[dã]
over (across the top of)	**par dessus** ... (prep)	[par dəsy]

5. Function words. Adverbs. Part 1

Where? (at, in)	**Où?**	[u]
here (adv)	**ici** (adv)	[isi]
there (adv)	**là-bas** (adv)	[laba]
somewhere (to be)	**quelque part** (adv)	[kɛlkə par]
nowhere (not anywhere)	**nulle part** (adv)	[nyl par]
by (near, beside)	**près de** ... (prep)	[prɛ də]
by the window	**près de la fenêtre**	[prɛdə la fənɛtr]
Where (to)?	**Où?**	[u]
here (e.g., come ~!)	**ici** (adv)	[isi]
there (e.g., to go ~)	**là-bas** (adv)	[laba]
from here (adv)	**d'ici** (adv)	[disi]
from there (adv)	**de là-bas** (adv)	[də laba]
close (adv)	**près** (adv)	[prɛ]
far (adv)	**loin** (adv)	[lwɛ̃]
near (e.g., ~ Paris)	**près de** ...	[prɛ də]
nearby (adv)	**tout près** (adv)	[tu prɛ]
not far (adv)	**pas loin** (adv)	[pɑ lwɛ̃]
left (adj)	**gauche** (adj)	[goʃ]
on the left	**à gauche** (adv)	[agoʃ]
to the left	**à gauche** (adv)	[agoʃ]
right (adj)	**droit** (adj)	[drwa]
on the right	**à droite** (adv)	[adrwat]
to the right	**à droite** (adv)	[adrwat]
in front (adv)	**devant** (adv)	[dəvã]
front (as adj)	**de devant** (adj)	[də dəvã]
ahead (the kids ran ~)	**en avant** (adv)	[ɑn avã]
behind (adv)	**derrière** (adv)	[dɛrjɛr]
from behind	**par derrière** (adv)	[par dɛrjɛr]
back (towards the rear)	**en arrière** (adv)	[ɑn arjɛr]
middle	**milieu** (m)	[miljø]
in the middle	**au milieu** (adv)	[omiljø]

at the side	de côté (adv)	[də kote]
everywhere (adv)	partout (adv)	[partu]
around (in all directions)	autour (adv)	[otur]

from inside	de l'intérieur	[də lɛ̃terjœr]
somewhere (to go)	quelque part (adv)	[kɛlkə par]
straight (directly)	tout droit (adv)	[tu drwa]
back (e.g., come ~)	en arrière (adv)	[ɑn arjɛr]

| from anywhere | de quelque part | [də kɛlkə par] |
| from somewhere | de quelque part | [də kɛlkə par] |

firstly (adv)	premièrement (adv)	[prəmjɛrmɑ̃]
secondly (adv)	deuxièmement (adv)	[døzjɛmmɑ̃]
thirdly (adv)	troisièmement (adv)	[trwazjɛmmɑ̃]

suddenly (adv)	soudain (adv)	[sudɛ̃]
at first (at the beginning)	au début (adv)	[odeby]
for the first time	pour la première fois	[pur la prəmjɛr fwa]
long before ...	bien avant ...	[bjɛn avɑ̃]
anew (over again)	de nouveau (adv)	[də nuvo]
for good (adv)	pour toujours (adv)	[pur tuʒur]

never (adv)	jamais (adv)	[ʒamɛ]
again (adv)	de nouveau, encore (adv)	[də nuvo], [ɑ̃kɔr]
now (adv)	maintenant (adv)	[mɛ̃tnɑ̃]
often (adv)	souvent (adv)	[suvɑ̃]
then (adv)	alors (adv)	[alɔr]
urgently (quickly)	d'urgence (adv)	[dyrʒɑ̃s]
usually (adv)	d'habitude (adv)	[dabityd]

by the way, ...	à propos, ...	[aprɔpo]
possible (that is ~)	c'est possible	[sepɔsibl]
probably (adv)	probablement (adv)	[prɔbabləmɑ̃]
maybe (adv)	peut-être (adv)	[pøtɛtr]
besides ...	en plus, ...	[ɑ̃plys]
that's why ...	c'est pourquoi ...	[se purkwa]
in spite of ...	malgré ...	[malgre]
thanks to ...	grâce à ...	[gras ɑ]

what (pron.)	quoi (pron)	[kwa]
that (conj.)	que (conj)	[kə]
something	quelque chose (pron)	[kɛlkə ʃoz]
anything (something)	quelque chose (pron)	[kɛlkə ʃoz]
nothing	rien	[rjɛ̃]

who (pron.)	qui (pron)	[ki]
someone	quelqu'un (pron)	[kɛlkœ̃]
somebody	quelqu'un (pron)	[kɛlkœ̃]

| nobody | personne (pron) | [pɛrsɔn] |
| nowhere (a voyage to ~) | nulle part (adv) | [nyl par] |

| nobody's | de personne | [də pɛrsɔn] |
| somebody's | de n'importe qui | [də nɛ̃pɔrt ki] |

so (I'm ~ glad)	comme ça (adv)	[kɔmsa]
also (as well)	également (adv)	[egalmɑ̃]
too (as well)	aussi (adv)	[osi]

6. Function words. Adverbs. Part 2

Why?	Pourquoi?	[purkwa]
for some reason	pour une certaine raison	pur yn sɛrtɛn rɛzɔ̃
because ...	parce que ...	[parskə]
for some purpose	pour une raison quelconque	[pur yn rɛzɔ̃ kɛlkɔ̃k]

and	et (conj)	[e]
or	ou (conj)	[u]
but	mais (conj)	[mɛ]
for (e.g., ~ me)	pour ... (prep)	[pur]

too (~ many people)	trop (adv)	[tro]
only (exclusively)	seulement (adv)	[sœlmɑ̃]
exactly (adv)	précisément (adv)	[presizemɑ̃]
about (more or less)	près de ... (prep)	[prɛ də]

approximately (adv)	approximativement	[aprɔksimativmɑ̃]
approximate (adj)	approximatif (adj)	[aprɔksimatif]
almost (adv)	presque (adv)	[prɛsk]
the rest	reste (m)	[rɛst]

the other (second)	l'autre (adj)	[lotr]
other (different)	autre (adj)	[otr]
each (adj)	chaque (adj)	[ʃak]
any (no matter which)	n'importe quel (adj)	[nɛ̃pɔrt kɛl]
many, much (a lot of)	beaucoup (adv)	[boku]
many people	beaucoup de gens	[boku də ʒɑ̃]
all (everyone)	tous	[tus]

in return for ...	en échange de ...	[ɑn eʃɑʒ də ...]
in exchange (adv)	en échange (adv)	[ɑn eʃɑʒ]
by hand (made)	à la main (adv)	[alamɛ̃]
hardly (negative opinion)	peu probable	[pø prɔbabl]

probably (adv)	probablement (adv)	[prɔbabləmɑ̃]
on purpose (intentionally)	exprès (adv)	[ɛksprɛ]
by accident (adv)	par accident (adv)	[par aksidɑ̃]

very (adv)	très (adv)	[trɛ]
for example (adv)	par exemple (adv)	[par ɛgzɑ̃p]
between	entre ... (prep)	[ɑ̃tr]

among	**parmi** ... (prep)	[parmi]
so much (such a lot)	**autant** (adv)	[otɑ̃]
especially (adv)	**surtout** (adv)	[syrtu]

T&P BOOKS

NUMBERS.
MISCELLANEOUS

T&P Books Publishing

0 zero	**zéro**	[zero]
1 one	**un**	[œ̃]
2 two	**deux**	[dø]
3 three	**trois**	[trwa]
4 four	**quatre**	[katr]
5 five	**cinq**	[sɛ̃k]
6 six	**six**	[sis]
7 seven	**sept**	[sɛt]
8 eight	**huit**	[ɥit]
9 nine	**neuf**	[nœf]
10 ten	**dix**	[dis]
11 eleven	**onze**	[ɔ̃z]
12 twelve	**douze**	[duz]
13 thirteen	**treize**	[trɛz]
14 fourteen	**quatorze**	[katɔrz]
15 fifteen	**quinze**	[kɛ̃z]
16 sixteen	**seize**	[sɛz]
17 seventeen	**dix-sept**	[disɛt]
18 eighteen	**dix-huit**	[dizɥit]
19 nineteen	**dix-neuf**	[diznœf]
20 twenty	**vingt**	[vɛ̃]
21 twenty-one	**vingt et un**	[vɛ̃teœ̃]
22 twenty-two	**vingt-deux**	[vɛ̃tdø]
23 twenty-three	**vingt-trois**	[vɛ̃trwa]
30 thirty	**trente**	[trɑ̃t]
31 thirty-one	**trente et un**	[trɑ̃teœ̃]
32 thirty-two	**trente-deux**	[trɑ̃t dø]
33 thirty-three	**trente-trois**	[trɑ̃t trwa]
40 forty	**quarante**	[karɑ̃t]
41 forty-one	**quarante et un**	[karɑ̃teœ̃]
42 forty-two	**quarante-deux**	[karɑ̃t dø]
43 forty-three	**quarante-trois**	[karɑ̃t trwa]
50 fifty	**cinquante**	[sɛ̃kɑ̃t]
51 fifty-one	**cinquante et un**	[sɛ̃kɑ̃teœ̃]
52 fifty-two	**cinquante-deux**	[sɛ̃kɑ̃t dø]
53 fifty-three	**cinquante-trois**	[sɛ̃kɑ̃t trwa]
60 sixty	**soixante**	[swasɑ̃t]

61 sixty-one	**soixante et un**	[swasɑ̃teœ̃]
62 sixty-two	**soixante-deux**	[swasɑ̃t dø]
63 sixty-three	**soixante-trois**	[swasɑ̃t trwa]

70 seventy	**soixante-dix**	[swasɑ̃tdis]
71 seventy-one	**soixante et onze**	[swasɑ̃te ɔ̃z]
72 seventy-two	**soixante-douze**	[swasɑ̃t duz]
73 seventy-three	**soixante-treize**	[swasɑ̃t trɛz]

80 eighty	**quatre-vingts**	[katrəvɛ̃]
81 eighty-one	**quatre-vingt et un**	[katrəvɛ̃teœ̃]
82 eighty-two	**quatre-vingt deux**	[katrəvɛ̃ dø]
83 eighty-three	**quatre-vingt trois**	[katrəvɛ̃ trwa]

90 ninety	**quatre-vingt-dix**	[katrəvɛ̃dis]
91 ninety-one	**quatre-vingt et onze**	[katrəvɛ̃ teɔ̃z]
92 ninety-two	**quatre-vingt-douze**	[katrəvɛ̃ duz]
93 ninety-three	**quatre-vingt-treize**	[katrəvɛ̃ trɛz]

8. Cardinal numbers. Part 2

100 one hundred	**cent**	[sɑ̃]
200 two hundred	**deux cents**	[dø sɑ̃]
300 three hundred	**trois cents**	[trwa sɑ̃]
400 four hundred	**quatre cents**	[katr sɑ̃]
500 five hundred	**cinq cents**	[sɛ̃k sɑ̃]

600 six hundred	**six cents**	[si sɑ̃]
700 seven hundred	**sept cents**	[sɛt sɑ̃]
800 eight hundred	**huit cents**	[ɥi sɑ̃]
900 nine hundred	**neuf cents**	[nœf sɑ̃]

1000 one thousand	**mille**	[mil]
2000 two thousand	**deux mille**	[dø mil]
3000 three thousand	**trois mille**	[trwa mil]
10000 ten thousand	**dix mille**	[di mil]
one hundred thousand	**cent mille**	[sɑ̃ mil]
million	**million** (m)	[miljɔ̃]
billion	**milliard** (m)	[miljar]

9. Ordinal numbers

first (adj)	**premier** (adj)	[prəmje]
second (adj)	**deuxième** (adj)	[døzjɛm]
third (adj)	**troisième** (adj)	[trwazjɛm]
fourth (adj)	**quatrième** (adj)	[katrijɛm]
fifth (adj)	**cinquième** (adj)	[sɛ̃kjɛm]
sixth (adj)	**sixième** (adj)	[sizjɛm]

seventh (adj)	septième (adj)	[sɛtjɛm]
eighth (adj)	huitième (adj)	[ɥitjɛm]
ninth (adj)	neuvième (adj)	[nœvjɛm]
tenth (adj)	dixième (adj)	[dizjɛm]

COLOURS. UNITS OF MEASUREMENT

T&P Books Publishing

10. Colors

color	**couleur** (f)	[kulœr]
shade (tint)	**teinte** (f)	[tɛ̃t]
hue	**ton** (m)	[tɔ̃]
rainbow	**arc-en-ciel** (m)	[arkɑ̃sjɛl]

white (adj)	**blanc** (adj)	[blɑ̃]
black (adj)	**noir** (adj)	[nwar]
gray (adj)	**gris** (adj)	[gri]

green (adj)	**vert** (adj)	[vɛr]
yellow (adj)	**jaune** (adj)	[ʒon]
red (adj)	**rouge** (adj)	[ruʒ]
blue (adj)	**bleu** (adj)	[blø]
light blue (adj)	**bleu clair** (adj)	[blø klɛr]
pink (adj)	**rose** (adj)	[roz]
orange (adj)	**orange** (adj)	[ɔrɑ̃ʒ]
violet (adj)	**violet** (adj)	[vjɔlɛ]
brown (adj)	**brun** (adj)	[brœ̃]

golden (adj)	**d'or** (adj)	[dɔr]
silvery (adj)	**argenté** (adj)	[arʒɑ̃te]
beige (adj)	**beige** (adj)	[bɛʒ]
cream (adj)	**crème** (adj)	[krɛm]
turquoise (adj)	**turquoise** (adj)	[tyrkwaz]
cherry red (adj)	**rouge cerise** (adj)	[ruʒ səriz]
lilac (adj)	**lilas** (adj)	[lila]
crimson (adj)	**framboise** (adj)	[frɑ̃bwaz]

light (adj)	**clair** (adj)	[klɛr]
dark (adj)	**foncé** (adj)	[fɔ̃se]
bright, vivid (adj)	**vif** (adj)	[vif]

colored (pencils)	**de couleur** (adj)	[də kulœr]
color (e.g., ~ film)	**en couleurs** (adj)	[ɑ̃ kulœr]
black-and-white (adj)	**noir et blanc** (adj)	[nwar e blɑ̃]
plain (one-colored)	**unicolore** (adj)	[ynikɔlɔr]
multicolored (adj)	**multicolore** (adj)	[myltikɔlɔr]

11. Units of measurement

weight	**poids** (m)	[pwa]
length	**longueur** (f)	[lɔ̃gœr]

width	largeur (f)	[larʒœr]
height	hauteur (f)	[otœr]
depth	profondeur (f)	[prɔfɔ̃dœr]
volume	volume (m)	[vɔlym]
area	aire (f)	[ɛr]

gram	gramme (m)	[gram]
milligram	milligramme (m)	[miligram]
kilogram	kilogramme (m)	[kilɔgram]
ton	tonne (f)	[tɔn]
pound	livre (f)	[livr]
ounce	once (f)	[ɔ̃s]

meter	mètre (m)	[mɛtr]
millimeter	millimètre (m)	[milimɛtr]
centimeter	centimètre (m)	[sɑ̃timɛtr]
kilometer	kilomètre (m)	[kilɔmɛtr]
mile	mille (m)	[mil]

inch	pouce (m)	[pus]
foot	pied (m)	[pje]
yard	yard (m)	[jard]

square meter	mètre (m) carré	[mɛtr kare]
hectare	hectare (m)	[ɛktar]
liter	litre (m)	[litr]
degree	degré (m)	[dəgre]
volt	volt (m)	[vɔlt]
ampere	ampère (m)	[ɑ̃pɛr]
horsepower	cheval-vapeur (m)	[ʃəvalvapœr]

quantity	quantité (f)	[kɑ̃tite]
a little bit of ...	un peu de ...	[œ̃ pø də]
half	moitié (f)	[mwatje]
dozen	douzaine (f)	[duzɛn]
piece (item)	pièce (f)	[pjɛs]

| size | dimension (f) | [dimɑ̃sjɔ̃] |
| scale (map ~) | échelle (f) | [eʃɛl] |

minimal (adj)	minimal (adj)	[minimal]
the smallest (adj)	le plus petit (adj)	[lə ply pəti]
medium (adj)	moyen (adj)	[mwajɛ̃]
maximal (adj)	maximal (adj)	[maksimal]
the largest (adj)	le plus grand (adj)	[lə ply grɑ̃]

12. Containers

| canning jar (glass ~) | bocal (m) en verre | [bɔkal ɑ̃ vɛr] |
| can | boîte, canette (f) | [bwat], [kanɛt] |

bucket	**seau** (m)	[so]
barrel	**tonneau** (m)	[tɔno]
wash basin (e.g., plastic ~)	**bassine, cuvette** (f)	[basin], [kyvɛt]
tank (100 - 200L water ~)	**cuve** (f)	[kyv]
hip flask	**flasque** (f)	[flask]
jerrycan	**jerrican** (m)	[ʒerikan]
tank (e.g., tank car)	**citerne** (f)	[sitɛrn]
mug	**tasse** (f), **mug** (m)	[tɑs], [mʌg]
cup (of coffee, etc.)	**tasse** (f)	[tɑs]
saucer	**soucoupe** (f)	[sukup]
glass (tumbler)	**verre** (m)	[vɛr]
wine glass	**verre** (m) **à vin**	[vɛr ɑ vɛ̃]
stock pot (soup pot)	**faitout** (m)	[fɛtu]
bottle (~ of wine)	**bouteille** (f)	[butɛj]
neck (of the bottle, etc.)	**goulot** (m)	[gulo]
carafe	**carafe** (f)	[karaf]
pitcher	**pichet** (m)	[piʃɛ]
vessel (container)	**récipient** (m)	[resipjɑ̃]
pot (crock, stoneware ~)	**pot** (m)	[po]
vase	**vase** (m)	[vaz]
bottle (perfume ~)	**flacon** (m)	[flakɔ̃]
vial, small bottle	**fiole** (f)	[fjɔl]
tube (of toothpaste)	**tube** (m)	[tyb]
sack (bag)	**sac** (m)	[sak]
bag (paper ~, plastic ~)	**sac** (m)	[sak]
pack (of cigarettes, etc.)	**paquet** (m)	[pakɛ]
box (e.g., shoebox)	**boîte** (f)	[bwat]
crate	**caisse** (f)	[kɛs]
basket	**panier** (m)	[panje]

MAIN VERBS

T&P Books Publishing

13. The most important verbs. Part 1

to advise (vt)	**conseiller** (vt)	[kɔ̃seje]
to agree (say yes)	**être d'accord**	[ɛtr dakɔr]
to answer (vi, vt)	**répondre** (vi, vt)	[repɔ̃dr]
to apologize (vi)	**s'excuser** (vp)	[sɛkskyze]
to arrive (vi)	**venir** (vi)	[vənir]
to ask (~ oneself)	**demander** (vt)	[dəmɑ̃de]
to ask (~ sb to do sth)	**demander** (vt)	[dəmɑ̃de]
to be (vi)	**être** (vi)	[ɛtr]
to be afraid	**avoir peur**	[avwar pœr]
to be hungry	**avoir faim**	[avwar fɛ̃]
to be interested in ...	**s'intéresser** (vp)	[sɛ̃terese]
to be needed	**être nécessaire**	[ɛtr nesesɛr]
to be surprised	**s'étonner** (vp)	[setɔne]
to be thirsty	**avoir soif**	[avwar swaf]
to begin (vt)	**commencer** (vt)	[kɔmɑ̃se]
to belong to ...	**appartenir à ...**	[apartənir a]
to boast (vi)	**se vanter** (vp)	[sə vɑ̃te]
to break (split into pieces)	**casser** (vt)	[kase]
to call (~ for help)	**appeler** (vt)	[aple]
can (v aux)	**pouvoir** (v aux)	[puvwar]
to catch (vt)	**attraper** (vt)	[atrape]
to change (vt)	**changer** (vt)	[ʃɑ̃ʒe]
to choose (select)	**choisir** (vt)	[ʃwazir]
to come down (the stairs)	**descendre** (vi)	[desɑ̃dr]
to compare (vt)	**comparer** (vt)	[kɔ̃pare]
to complain (vi, vt)	**se plaindre** (vp)	[sə plɛ̃dr]
to confuse (mix up)	**confondre** (vt)	[kɔ̃fɔ̃dr]
to continue (vt)	**continuer** (vt)	[kɔ̃tinɥe]
to control (vt)	**contrôler** (vt)	[kɔ̃trole]
to cook (dinner)	**préparer** (vt)	[prepare]
to cost (vt)	**coûter** (vt)	[kute]
to count (add up)	**compter** (vi, vt)	[kɔ̃te]
to count on ...	**compter sur ...**	[kɔ̃te syr]
to create (vt)	**créer** (vt)	[kree]
to cry (weep)	**pleurer** (vi)	[plœre]

14. The most important verbs. Part 2

to deceive (vi, vt)	tromper (vt)	[trɔ̃pe]
to decorate (tree, street)	décorer (vt)	[dekɔre]
to defend (a country, etc.)	défendre (vt)	[defɑ̃dr]
to demand (request firmly)	exiger (vt)	[ɛgziʒe]
to dig (vt)	creuser (vt)	[krøze]

to discuss (vt)	discuter (vt)	[diskyte]
to do (vt)	faire (vt)	[fɛr]
to doubt (have doubts)	douter (vt)	[dute]
to drop (let fall)	faire tomber	[fɛr tɔ̃be]
to enter	entrer (vi)	[ɑ̃tre]
(room, house, etc.)		

to excuse (forgive)	excuser (vt)	[ɛkskyze]
to exist (vi)	exister (vi)	[ɛgziste]
to expect (foresee)	prévoir (vt)	[prevwar]

to explain (vt)	expliquer (vt)	[ɛksplike]
to fall (vi)	tomber (vi)	[tɔ̃be]

to find (vt)	trouver (vt)	[truve]
to finish (vt)	finir (vt)	[finir]
to fly (vi)	voler (vi)	[vɔle]

to follow ... (come after)	suivre (vt)	[sɥivr]
to forget (vi, vt)	oublier (vt)	[ublije]

to forgive (vt)	pardonner (vt)	[pardɔne]
to give (vt)	donner (vt)	[dɔne]

to give a hint	donner un indice	[dɔne ynɛ̃dis]
to go (on foot)	aller (vi)	[ale]

to go for a swim	se baigner (vp)	[sə beɲe]
to go out (for dinner, etc.)	sortir (vi)	[sɔrtir]
to guess (the answer)	deviner (vt)	[dəvine]

to have (vt)	avoir (vt)	[avwar]
to have breakfast	prendre le petit déjeuner	[prɑ̃dr ləpti deʒœne]
to have dinner	dîner (vi)	[dine]

to have lunch	déjeuner (vi)	[deʒœne]
to hear (vt)	entendre (vt)	[ɑ̃tɑ̃dr]

to help (vt)	aider (vt)	[ede]
to hide (vt)	cacher (vt)	[kaʃe]
to hope (vi, vt)	espérer (vi)	[ɛspere]
to hunt (vi, vt)	chasser (vi, vt)	[ʃase]
to hurry (vi)	être pressé	[ɛtr prese]

15. The most important verbs. Part 3

to inform (vt)	**informer** (vt)	[ɛ̃fɔrme]
to insist (vi, vt)	**insister** (vi)	[ɛ̃siste]
to insult (vt)	**insulter** (vt)	[ɛ̃sylte]
to invite (vt)	**inviter** (vt)	[ɛ̃vite]
to joke (vi)	**plaisanter** (vi)	[plɛzɑ̃te]
to keep (vt)	**garder** (vt)	[garde]
to keep silent	**rester silencieux**	[rɛste silɑ̃sjø]
to kill (vt)	**tuer** (vt)	[tɥe]
to know (sb)	**connaître** (vt)	[kɔnɛtr]
to know (sth)	**savoir** (vt)	[savwar]

to laugh (vi)	**rire** (vi)	[rir]
to liberate (city, etc.)	**libérer** (vt)	[libere]
to like (I like ...)	**plaire** (vt)	[plɛr]
to look for ... (search)	**chercher** (vt)	[ʃɛrʃe]
to love (sb)	**aimer** (vt)	[eme]
to make a mistake	**se tromper** (vp)	[sə trɔ̃pe]
to manage, to run	**diriger** (vt)	[diriʒe]
to mean (signify)	**signifier** (vt)	[siɲifje]
to mention (talk about)	**mentionner** (vt)	[mɑ̃sjɔne]
to miss (school, etc.)	**manquer** (vt)	[mɑ̃ke]
to notice (see)	**apercevoir** (vt)	[apɛrsəvwar]

to object (vi, vt)	**objecter** (vt)	[ɔbʒɛkte]
to observe (see)	**observer** (vt)	[ɔpsɛrve]
to open (vt)	**ouvrir** (vt)	[uvrir]
to order (meal, etc.)	**commander** (vt)	[kɔmɑ̃de]
to order (mil.)	**ordonner** (vt)	[ɔrdɔne]
to own (possess)	**posséder** (vt)	[pɔsede]

to participate (vi)	**participer à ...**	[partisipe a]
to pay (vi, vt)	**payer** (vi, vt)	[peje]
to permit (vt)	**permettre** (vt)	[pɛrmɛtr]
to plan (vt)	**planifier** (vt)	[planifje]
to play (children)	**jouer** (vt)	[ʒwe]
to pray (vi, vt)	**prier** (vt)	[prije]
to prefer (vt)	**préférer** (vt)	[prefere]
to promise (vt)	**promettre** (vt)	[prɔmɛtr]
to pronounce (vt)	**prononcer** (vt)	[prɔnɔ̃se]
to propose (vt)	**proposer** (vt)	[prɔpoze]
to punish (vt)	**punir** (vt)	[pynir]

16. The most important verbs. Part 4

to read (vi, vt)	**lire** (vi, vt)	[lir]
to recommend (vt)	**recommander** (vt)	[rəkɔmɑ̃de]
to refuse (vi, vt)	**se refuser** (vp)	[sə rəfyze]

| to regret (be sorry) | regretter (vt) | [rəgrɛte] |
| to rent (sth from sb) | louer (vt) | [lwe] |

to repeat (say again)	répéter (vt)	[repete]
to reserve, to book	réserver (vt)	[rezɛrve]
to run (vi)	courir (vt)	[kurir]
to save (rescue)	sauver (vt)	[sove]
to say (~ thank you)	dire (vt)	[dir]

to scold (vt)	gronder (vt),	[grɔ̃de],
	réprimander (vt)	[reprimɑ̃de]
to see (vt)	voir (vt)	[vwar]
to sell (vt)	vendre (vt)	[vɑ̃dr]
to send (vt)	envoyer (vt)	[ɑ̃vwaje]
to shoot (vi)	tirer (vi)	[tire]

to shout (vi)	crier (vi)	[krije]
to show (vt)	montrer (vt)	[mɔ̃tre]
to sign (document)	signer (vt)	[siɲe]
to sit down (vi)	s'asseoir (vp)	[saswar]

to smile (vi)	sourire (vi)	[surir]
to speak (vi, vt)	parler (vi, vt)	[parle]
to steal (money, etc.)	voler (vt)	[vɔle]
to stop (for pause, etc.)	s'arrêter (vp)	[sarete]
to stop	cesser (vt)	[sese]
(please ~ calling me)		

to study (vt)	étudier (vt)	[etydje]
to swim (vi)	nager (vi)	[naʒe]
to take (vt)	prendre (vt)	[prɑ̃dr]
to think (vi, vt)	penser (vi, vt)	[pɑ̃se]
to threaten (vt)	menacer (vt)	[mənase]

to touch (with hands)	toucher (vt)	[tuʃe]
to translate (vt)	traduire (vt)	[tradɥir]
to trust (vt)	avoir confiance	[avwar kɔ̃fjɑ̃s]
to try (attempt)	essayer (vt)	[eseje]
to turn (e.g., ~ left)	tourner (vi)	[turne]

| to underestimate (vt) | sous-estimer (vt) | [suzɛstime] |
| to understand (vt) | comprendre (vt) | [kɔ̃prɑ̃dr] |

| to unite (vt) | réunir (vt) | [reynir] |
| to wait (vt) | attendre (vt) | [atɑ̃dr] |

to want (wish, desire)	vouloir (vt)	[vulwar]
to warn (vt)	avertir (vt)	[avɛrtir]
to work (vi)	travailler (vi)	[travaje]
to write (vt)	écrire (vt)	[ekrir]
to write down	prendre en note	[prɑ̃dr ɑ̃ nɔt]

TIME. CALENDAR

T&P Books Publishing

17. Weekdays

Monday	**lundi** (m)	[lœ̃di]
Tuesday	**mardi** (m)	[mardi]
Wednesday	**mercredi** (m)	[mɛrkrədi]
Thursday	**jeudi** (m)	[ʒødi]
Friday	**vendredi** (m)	[vãdrədi]
Saturday	**samedi** (m)	[samdi]
Sunday	**dimanche** (m)	[dimãʃ]

today (adv)	**aujourd'hui** (adv)	[oʒurdɥi]
tomorrow (adv)	**demain** (adv)	[dəmɛ̃]
the day after tomorrow	**après-demain** (adv)	[aprɛdmɛ̃]
yesterday (adv)	**hier** (adv)	[ijɛr]
the day before yesterday	**avant-hier** (adv)	[avãtjɛr]

day	**jour** (m)	[ʒur]
working day	**jour** (m) **ouvrable**	[ʒur uvrabl]
public holiday	**jour** (m) **férié**	[ʒur ferje]
day off	**jour** (m) **de repos**	[ʒur də rəpo]
weekend	**week-end** (m)	[wikɛnd]

all day long	**toute la journée**	[tut la ʒurne]
the next day (adv)	**le lendemain**	[lãdmɛ̃]
two days ago	**il y a 2 jours**	[ilja də ʒur]
the day before	**la veille**	[la vɛj]
daily (adj)	**quotidien** (adj)	[kɔtidjɛ̃]
every day (adv)	**tous les jours**	[tu le ʒur]

week	**semaine** (f)	[səmɛn]
last week (adv)	**la semaine dernière**	[la səmɛn dɛrnjɛr]
next week (adv)	**la semaine prochaine**	[la səmɛn prɔʃɛn]
weekly (adj)	**hebdomadaire** (adj)	[ɛbdɔmadɛr]
every week (adv)	**chaque semaine**	[ʃak səmɛn]
twice a week	**2 fois par semaine**	[dø fwa par səmɛn]
every Tuesday	**tous les mardis**	[tu le mardi]

18. Hours. Day and night

morning	**matin** (m)	[matɛ̃]
in the morning	**le matin**	[lə matɛ̃]
noon, midday	**midi** (m)	[midi]
in the afternoon	**dans l'après-midi**	[dã laprɛmidi]
evening	**soir** (m)	[swar]

in the evening	le soir	[lə swar]
night	nuit (f)	[nyi]
at night	la nuit	[la nyi]
midnight	minuit (f)	[minyi]
second	seconde (f)	[səgɔ̃d]
minute	minute (f)	[minyt]
hour	heure (f)	[œr]
half an hour	demi-heure (f)	[dəmijœr]
a quarter-hour	un quart d'heure	[œ̃ kar dœr]
fifteen minutes	quinze minutes	[kɛ̃z minyt]
24 hours	vingt-quatre heures	[vɛ̃tkatr œr]
sunrise	lever (m) du soleil	[ləve dy sɔlɛj]
dawn	aube (f)	[ob]
early morning	point (m) du jour	[pwɛ̃ dy ʒur]
sunset	coucher (m) du soleil	[kuʃe dy sɔlɛj]
early in the morning	tôt le matin	[to lə matɛ̃]
this morning	ce matin	[sə matɛ̃]
tomorrow morning	demain matin	[dəmɛ̃ matɛ̃]
this afternoon	cet après-midi	[sɛt aprɛmidi]
in the afternoon	dans l'après-midi	[dɑ̃ laprɛmidi]
tomorrow afternoon	demain après-midi	[dəmɛn aprɛmidi]
tonight (this evening)	ce soir	[sə swar]
tomorrow night	demain soir	[dəmɛ̃ swar]
at 3 o'clock sharp	à trois heures précises	[ɑ trwa zœr presiz]
about 4 o'clock	autour de quatre heures	[otur də katr œr]
by 12 o'clock	vers midi	[vɛr midi]
in 20 minutes	dans 20 minutes	[dɑ̃ vɛ̃ minyt]
in an hour	dans une heure	[dɑ̃zyn œr]
on time (adv)	à temps	[ɑ tɑ̃]
a quarter of …	… moins le quart	[mwɛ̃ lə kar]
within an hour	en une heure	[ɑnyn œr]
every 15 minutes	tous les quarts d'heure	[tu le kar dœr]
round the clock	24 heures sur 24	[vɛ̃tkatr œr syr vɛ̃tkatr]

19. Months. Seasons

January	janvier (m)	[ʒɑ̃vje]
February	février (m)	[fevrije]
March	mars (m)	[mars]
April	avril (m)	[avril]
May	mai (m)	[mɛ]
June	juin (m)	[ʒɥɛ̃]

July	**juillet** (m)	[ʒɥijɛ]
August	**août** (m)	[ut]
September	**septembre** (m)	[separemã]
October	**octobre** (m)	[ɔktɔbr]
November	**novembre** (m)	[nɔvãbr]
December	**décembre** (m)	[desãbr]
spring	**printemps** (m)	[prɛ̃tã]
in spring	**au printemps**	[oprɛ̃tã]
spring (as adj)	**de printemps** (adj)	[də prɛ̃tã]
summer	**été** (m)	[ete]
in summer	**en été**	[ɑn ete]
summer (as adj)	**d'été** (adj)	[dete]
fall	**automne** (m)	[otɔn]
in fall	**en automne**	[ɑn otɔn]
fall (as adj)	**d'automne** (adj)	[dotɔn]
winter	**hiver** (m)	[ivɛr]
in winter	**en hiver**	[ɑn ivɛr]
winter (as adj)	**d'hiver** (adj)	[divɛr]
month	**mois** (m)	[mwa]
this month	**ce mois**	[sə mwa]
next month	**le mois prochain**	[lə mwa prɔʃɛ̃]
last month	**le mois dernier**	[lə mwa dɛrnje]
a month ago	**il y a un mois**	[ilja œ̃ mwa]
in a month (a month later)	**dans un mois**	[dãzœn mwa]
in 2 months (2 months later)	**dans 2 mois**	[dã dø mwa]
the whole month	**tout le mois**	[tu lə mwa]
all month long	**tout un mois**	[tutœ̃ mwa]
monthly (~ magazine)	**mensuel** (adj)	[mãsɥɛl]
monthly (adv)	**mensuellement**	[mãsɥɛlmã]
every month	**chaque mois**	[ʃak mwa]
twice a month	**2 fois par mois**	[dø fwa par mwa]
year	**année** (f)	[ane]
this year	**cette année**	[sɛt ane]
next year	**l'année prochaine**	[lane prɔʃɛn]
last year	**l'année dernière**	[lane dɛrnjɛr]
a year ago	**il y a un an**	[ilja œ̃nã]
in a year	**dans un an**	[dãzœn ã]
in two years	**dans deux ans**	[dã dø zã]
the whole year	**toute l'année**	[tut lane]
all year long	**toute une année**	[tutyn ane]
every year	**chaque année**	[ʃak ane]
annual (adj)	**annuel** (adj)	[anɥɛl]

annually (adv)	**annuellement**	[anɥɛlmɑ̃]
4 times a year	**quatre fois par an**	[katr fwa parɑ̃]
date (e.g., today's ~)	**date** (f)	[dat]
date (e.g., ~ of birth)	**date** (f)	[dat]
calendar	**calendrier** (m)	[kalɑ̃drije]
half a year	**six mois**	[si mwa]
six months	**semestre** (m)	[səmɛstr]
season (summer, etc.)	**saison** (f)	[sɛzɔ̃]
century	**siècle** (m)	[sjɛkl]

T&P BOOKS

TRAVEL. HOTEL

T&P Books Publishing

20. Trip. Travel

tourism, travel	**tourisme** (m)	[turism]
tourist	**touriste** (m)	[turist]
trip, voyage	**voyage** (m)	[vwajaʒ]
adventure	**aventure** (f)	[avɑ̃tyr]
trip, journey	**voyage** (m)	[vwajaʒ]
vacation	**vacances** (f pl)	[vakɑ̃s]
to be on vacation	**être en vacances**	[ɛtr ɑ̃ vakɑ̃s]
rest	**repos** (m)	[rəpo]
train	**train** (m)	[trɛ̃]
by train	**en train**	[ɑ̃ trɛ̃]
airplane	**avion** (m)	[avjɔ̃]
by airplane	**en avion**	[ɑn avjɔ̃]
by car	**en voiture**	[ɑ̃ vwatyr]
by ship	**en bateau**	[ɑ̃ bato]
luggage	**bagage** (m)	[bagaʒ]
suitcase	**malle** (f)	[mal]
luggage cart	**chariot** (m)	[ʃarjo]
passport	**passeport** (m)	[pɑspɔr]
visa	**visa** (m)	[viza]
ticket	**ticket** (m)	[tikɛ]
air ticket	**billet** (m) **d'avion**	[bijɛ davjɔ̃]
guidebook	**guide** (m)	[gid]
map (tourist ~)	**carte** (f)	[kart]
area (rural ~)	**région** (f)	[reʒjɔ̃]
place, site	**endroit** (m)	[ɑ̃drwa]
exotica (n)	**exotisme** (m)	[ɛgzɔtism]
exotic (adj)	**exotique** (adj)	[ɛgzɔtik]
amazing (adj)	**étonnant** (adj)	[etɔnɑ̃]
group	**groupe** (m)	[grup]
excursion, sightseeing tour	**excursion** (f)	[ɛkskyrsjɔ̃]
guide (person)	**guide** (m)	[gid]

21. Hotel

hotel	**hôtel** (m)	[otɛl]
motel	**motel** (m)	[mɔtɛl]

three-star	3 étoiles	[trwa zetwal]
five-star	5 étoiles	[sɛ̆k etwal]
to stay (in hotel, etc.)	descendre (vi)	[desɑ̃dr]

room	chambre (f)	[ʃɑ̃br]
single room	chambre (f) simple	[ʃɑ̃br sɛ̃pl]
double room	chambre (f) double	[ʃɑ̃br dubl]
to book a room	réserver une chambre	[rezɛrve yn ʃɑ̃br]

| half board | demi-pension (f) | [dəmipɑ̃sjɔ̃] |
| full board | pension (f) complète | [pɑ̃sjɔ̃ kɔ̃plɛt] |

with bath	avec une salle de bain	[avɛk yn saldəbɛ̃]
with shower	avec une douche	[avɛk yn duʃ]
satellite television	télévision (f) par satellite	[televizjɔ̃ par satelit]
air-conditioner	climatiseur (m)	[klimatizœr]
towel	serviette (f)	[sɛrvjɛt]
key	clé, clef (f)	[kle]

administrator	administrateur (m)	[administratœr]
chambermaid	femme (f) de chambre	[fam də ʃɑ̃br]
porter, bellboy	porteur (m)	[pɔrtœr]
doorman	portier (m)	[pɔrtje]

restaurant	restaurant (m)	[rɛstɔrɑ̃]
pub, bar	bar (m)	[bar]
breakfast	petit déjeuner (m)	[pəti deʒœne]
dinner	dîner (m)	[dine]
buffet	buffet (m)	[byfɛ]

| lobby | hall (m) | [ol] |
| elevator | ascenseur (m) | [asɑ̃sœr] |

| DO NOT DISTURB | PRIÈRE DE NE PAS DÉRANGER | [prijɛr dənəpɑ derɑ̃ʒe] |
| NO SMOKING | DÉFENSE DE FUMER | [defɑ̃s də fyme] |

22. Sightseeing

monument	monument (m)	[mɔnymɑ̃]
fortress	forteresse (f)	[fɔrtərɛs]
palace	palais (m)	[palɛ]
castle	château (m)	[ʃato]
tower	tour (f)	[tur]
mausoleum	mausolée (m)	[mozɔle]

architecture	architecture (f)	[arʃitɛktyr]
medieval (adj)	médiéval (adj)	[medjeval]
ancient (adj)	ancien (adj)	[ɑ̃sjɛ̃]
national (adj)	national (adj)	[nasjɔnal]

well-known (adj)	connu (adj)	[kɔny]
tourist	touriste (m)	[turist]
guide (person)	guide (m)	[gid]
excursion, sightseeing tour	excursion (f)	[ɛkskyrsjɔ̃]
to show (vt)	montrer (vt)	[mɔ̃tre]
to tell (vt)	raconter (vt)	[rakɔ̃te]
to find (vt)	trouver (vt)	[truve]
to get lost (lose one's way)	se perdre (vp)	[sə pɛrdr]
map (e.g., subway ~)	plan (m)	[plɑ̃]
map (e.g., city ~)	carte (f)	[kart]
souvenir, gift	souvenir (m)	[suvnir]
gift shop	boutique (f) de souvenirs	[butik də suvnir]
to take pictures	prendre en photo	[prɑ̃dr ɑ̃ fɔto]
to have one's picture taken	se faire prendre en photo	[sə fɛr prɑ̃dr ɑ̃ fɔto]

T&P BOOKS

TRANSPORTATION

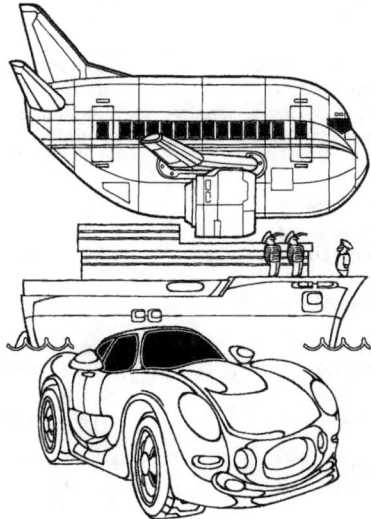

T&P Books Publishing

23. Airport

airport	**aéroport** (m)	[aeropɔr]
airplane	**avion** (m)	[avjɔ̃]
airline	**compagnie** (f) **aérienne**	[kɔ̃paɲi aerjɛn]
air traffic controller	**contrôleur** (m) **aérien**	[kɔ̃trolœr aerjɛ̃]

departure	**départ** (m)	[depar]
arrival	**arrivée** (f)	[arive]
to arrive (by plane)	**arriver** (vi)	[arive]

departure time	**temps** (m) **de départ**	[tɑ̃ də depar]
arrival time	**temps** (m) **d'arrivée**	[tɑ̃ darive]

to be delayed	**être retardé**	[ɛtr rətarde]
flight delay	**retard** (m) **de l'avion**	[rətar də lavjɔ̃]

information board	**tableau** (m) **d'informations**	[tablo dɛ̃formasjɔ̃]
information	**information** (f)	[ɛ̃formasjɔ̃]
to announce (vt)	**annoncer** (vt)	[anɔ̃se]
flight (e.g., next ~)	**vol** (m)	[vɔl]

customs	**douane** (f)	[dwan]
customs officer	**douanier** (m)	[dwanje]

customs declaration	**déclaration** (f) **de douane**	[deklarasjɔ̃ də dwan]
to fill out (vt)	**remplir** (vt)	[rɑ̃plir]
to fill out the declaration	**remplir la déclaration**	[rɑ̃plir la deklarasjɔ̃]
passport control	**contrôle** (m) **de passeport**	[kɔ̃trol də paspɔr]

luggage	**bagage** (m)	[bagaʒ]
hand luggage	**bagage** (m) **à main**	[bagaʒ a mɛ̃]
Lost Luggage Desk	**service des objets trouvés**	[sɛrvis de ɔbʒɛ truve]
luggage cart	**chariot** (m)	[ʃarjo]

landing	**atterrissage** (m)	[aterisaʒ]
landing strip	**piste** (f) **d'atterrissage**	[pist daterisaʒ]
to land (vi)	**atterrir** (vi)	[aterir]
airstairs	**escalier** (m) **d'avion**	[ɛskalje davjɔ̃]

check-in	**enregistrement** (m)	[ɑ̃rəʒistrəmɑ̃]
check-in desk	**comptoir** (m) **d'enregistrement**	[kɔ̃twar dɑ̃rəʒistrəmɑ̃]

to check-in (vi)	s'enregistrer (vp)	[sɑ̃rəʒistre]
boarding pass	carte (f) d'embarquement	[kart dɑ̃barkəmɑ̃]
departure gate	porte (f) d'embarquement	[pɔrt dɑ̃barkəmɑ̃]

transit	transit (m)	[trɑ̃zit]
to wait (vt)	attendre (vt)	[atɑ̃dr]
departure lounge	salle (f) d'attente	[sal datɑ̃t]
to see off	raccompagner (vt)	[rakɔ̃paɲe]
to say goodbye	dire au revoir	[dir ərəvwar]

24. Airplane

airplane	avion (m)	[avjɔ̃]
air ticket	billet (m) d'avion	[bijɛ davjɔ̃]
airline	compagnie (f) aérienne	[kɔ̃paɲi aerjɛn]
airport	aéroport (m)	[aeropɔr]
supersonic (adj)	supersonique (adj)	[sypɛrsɔnik]

captain	commandant (m) de bord	[kɔmɑ̃dɑ̃ də bɔr]
crew	équipage (m)	[ekipaʒ]
pilot	pilote (m)	[pilɔt]
flight attendant	hôtesse (f) de l'air	[otɛs də lɛr]
navigator	navigateur (m)	[navigatœr]

wings	ailes (f pl)	[ɛl]
tail	queue (f)	[kø]
cockpit	cabine (f)	[kabin]
engine	moteur (m)	[motœr]
undercarriage (landing gear)	train (m) d'atterrissage	[trɛ̃ daterisaʒ]
turbine	turbine (f)	[tyrbin]

propeller	hélice (f)	[elis]
black box	boîte (f) noire	[bwat nwar]
yoke (control column)	gouvernail (m)	[guvɛrnaj]
fuel	carburant (m)	[karbyrɑ̃]

safety card	consigne (f) de sécurité	[kɔ̃siɲ də sekyrite]
oxygen mask	masque (m) à oxygène	[mask a ɔksiʒɛn]
uniform	uniforme (m)	[yniform]
life vest	gilet (m) de sauvetage	[ʒilɛ də sovtaʒ]
parachute	parachute (m)	[paraʃyt]

takeoff	décollage (m)	[dekɔlaʒ]
to take off (vi)	décoller (vi)	[dekɔle]
runway	piste (f) de décollage	[pist dekɔlaʒ]

visibility	visibilité (f)	[vizibilite]
flight (act of flying)	vol (m)	[vɔl]
altitude	altitude (f)	[altityd]

air pocket	trou (m) d'air	[tru dɛr]
seat	place (f)	[plas]
headphones	écouteurs (m pl)	[ekutœr]
folding tray (tray table)	tablette (f)	[tablɛt]
airplane window	hublot (m)	[yblo]
aisle	couloir (m)	[kulwar]

25. Train

train	train (m)	[trɛ̃]
commuter train	train (m) de banlieue	[trɛ̃ də bɑ̃ljø]
express train	TGV (m)	[teʒeve]
diesel locomotive	locomotive (f) diesel	[lɔkɔmɔtiv djezɛl]
steam locomotive	locomotive (f) à vapeur	[lɔkɔmɔtiv ɑ vapœr]

| passenger car | wagon (m) | [vagɔ̃] |
| dining car | wagon-restaurant (m) | [vagɔ̃rɛstɔrɑ̃] |

rails	rails (m pl)	[raj]
railroad	chemin (m) de fer	[ʃəmɛ̃ də fɛr]
railway tie	traverse (f)	[travɛrs]

platform (railway ~)	quai (m)	[kɛ]
track (~ 1, 2, etc.)	voie (f)	[vwa]
semaphore	sémaphore (m)	[semafɔr]
station	station (f)	[stasjɔ̃]

engineer (train driver)	conducteur (m) de train	[kɔ̃dyktœr də trɛ̃]
porter (of luggage)	porteur (m)	[pɔrtœr]
car attendant	steward (m)	[stiwart]
passenger	passager (m)	[pɑsaʒe]
conductor (ticket inspector)	contrôleur (m)	[kɔ̃trolœr]

| corridor (in train) | couloir (m) | [kulwar] |
| emergency brake | frein (m) d'urgence | [frɛ̃ dyrʒɑ̃s] |

compartment	compartiment (m)	[kɔ̃partimɑ̃]
berth	couchette (f)	[kuʃɛt]
upper berth	couchette (f) d'en haut	[kuʃɛt dɛ̃ o]
lower berth	couchette (f) d'en bas	[kuʃɛt dɛ̃ba]
bed linen, bedding	linge (m) de lit	[lɛ̃ʒ də li]

ticket	ticket (m)	[tikɛ]
schedule	horaire (m)	[ɔrɛr]
information display	tableau (m) d'informations	[tablo dɛ̃fɔrmasjɔ̃]

| to leave, to depart | partir (vi) | [partir] |
| departure (of train) | départ (m) | [depar] |

to arrive (ab. train)	**arriver** (vi)	[arive]
arrival	**arrivée** (f)	[arive]

to arrive by train	**arriver en train**	[arive ɑ̃ trɛ̃]
to get on the train	**prendre le train**	[prɑ̃dr lə trɛ̃]
to get off the train	**descendre du train**	[desɑ̃dr dy trɛ̃]

train wreck	**accident** (m) **ferroviaire**	[aksidɑ̃ ferɔvjɛr]
to derail (vi)	**dérailler** (vi)	[deraje]

steam locomotive	**locomotive** (f) **à vapeur**	[lɔkɔmɔtiv a vapœr]
stoker, fireman	**chauffeur** (m)	[ʃofœr]
firebox	**chauffe** (f)	[ʃof]
coal	**charbon** (m)	[ʃarbɔ̃]

26. Ship

ship	**bateau** (m)	[bato]
vessel	**navire** (m)	[navir]

steamship	**bateau** (m) **à vapeur**	[bato a vapœr]
riverboat	**paquebot** (m)	[pakbo]
cruise ship	**bateau** (m) **de croisière**	[bato də krwazjɛr]
cruiser	**croiseur** (m)	[krwazœr]

yacht	**yacht** (m)	[jot]
tugboat	**remorqueur** (m)	[rəmɔrkœr]
barge	**péniche** (f)	[peniʃ]
ferry	**ferry** (m)	[feri]

sailing ship	**voilier** (m)	[vwalje]
brigantine	**brigantin** (m)	[brigɑ̃tɛ̃]

ice breaker	**brise-glace** (m)	[brizglas]
submarine	**sous-marin** (m)	[sumarɛ̃]

boat (flat-bottomed ~)	**canot** (m) **à rames**	[kano a ram]
dinghy	**dinghy** (m)	[diŋgi]
lifeboat	**canot** (m) **de sauvetage**	[kano də sovtaʒ]
motorboat	**canot** (m) **à moteur**	[kano a mɔtœr]

captain	**capitaine** (m)	[kapitɛn]
seaman	**matelot** (m)	[matlo]
sailor	**marin** (m)	[marɛ̃]
crew	**équipage** (m)	[ekipaʒ]

boatswain	**maître** (m) **d'équipage**	[mɛtr dekipaʒ]
ship's boy	**mousse** (m)	[mus]
cook	**cuisinier** (m) **du bord**	[kɥizinje dy bɔr]
ship's doctor	**médecin** (m) **de bord**	[medsɛ̃ də bɔr]

deck	pont (m)	[põ]
mast	mât (m)	[mɑ]
sail	voile (f)	[vwal]
hold	cale (f)	[kal]
bow (prow)	proue (f)	[pru]
stern	poupe (f)	[pup]
oar	rame (f)	[ram]
screw propeller	hélice (f)	[elis]
cabin	cabine (f)	[kabin]
wardroom	carré (m) des officiers	[kare dezɔfisje]
engine room	salle (f) des machines	[sal de maʃin]
bridge	passerelle (f)	[pɑsrɛl]
radio room	cabine (f) de T.S.F.	[kabin də teɛsɛf]
wave (radio)	onde (f)	[õd]
logbook	journal (m) de bord	[ʒurnal də bɔr]
spyglass	longue-vue (f)	[lõgvy]
bell	cloche (f)	[klɔʃ]
flag	pavillon (m)	[pavijõ]
rope (mooring ~)	grosse corde (f) tressée	[gros kɔrd trese]
knot (bowline, etc.)	nœud (m) marin	[nø marɛ̃]
deckrails	rampe (f)	[rɑ̃p]
gangway	passerelle (f)	[pɑsrɛl]
anchor	ancre (f)	[ɑ̃kr]
to weigh anchor	lever l'ancre	[ləve lɑ̃kr]
to drop anchor	jeter l'ancre	[ʒəte lɑ̃kr]
anchor chain	chaîne (f) d'ancrage	[ʃɛn dɑ̃kraʒ]
port (harbor)	port (m)	[pɔr]
quay, wharf	embarcadère (m)	[ɑ̃barkadɛr]
to berth (moor)	accoster (vi)	[akɔste]
to cast off	larguer les amarres	[large lezamar]
trip, voyage	voyage (m)	[vwajaʒ]
cruise (sea trip)	croisière (f)	[krwazjɛr]
course (route)	cap (m)	[kap]
route (itinerary)	itinéraire (m)	[itinerɛr]
fairway	chenal (m)	[ʃənal]
shallows	bas-fond (m)	[bafõ]
to run aground	échouer sur un bas-fond	[eʃwe syr œ̃ bafõ]
storm	tempête (f)	[tɑ̃pɛt]
signal	signal (m)	[siɲal]
to sink (vi)	sombrer (vi)	[sõbre]
Man overboard!	Un homme à la mer!	[ynɔm alamɛr]
SOS (distress signal)	SOS (m)	[ɛsoɛs]
ring buoy	bouée (f) de sauvetage	[bwe də sovtaʒ]

T&P BOOKS

CITY

T&P Books Publishing

27. Urban transportation

bus	**autobus** (m)	[otobys]
streetcar	**tramway** (m)	[tramwɛ]
trolley bus	**trolleybus** (m)	[trɔlɛbys]
route (of bus, etc.)	**itinéraire** (m)	[itinerɛr]
number (e.g., bus ~)	**numéro** (m)	[nymero]
to go by ...	**prendre** ...	[prãdr]
to get on (~ the bus)	**monter** (vi)	[mõte]
to get off ...	**descendre de** ...	[desãdr də]
stop (e.g., bus ~)	**arrêt** (m)	[arɛ]
next stop	**arrêt** (m) **prochain**	[arɛt prɔʃɛ̃]
terminus	**terminus** (m)	[tɛrminys]
schedule	**horaire** (m)	[ɔrɛr]
to wait (vt)	**attendre** (vt)	[atãdr]
ticket	**ticket** (m)	[tikɛ]
fare	**prix** (m) **du ticket**	[pri dy tikɛ]
cashier (ticket seller)	**caissier** (m)	[kesje]
ticket inspection	**contrôle** (m) **des tickets**	[kõtrol de tikɛ]
ticket inspector	**contrôleur** (m)	[kõtrolœr]
to be late (for ...)	**être en retard**	[ɛtr ã rətar]
to miss (~ the train, etc.)	**rater** (vt)	[rate]
to be in a hurry	**se dépêcher**	[sə depeʃe]
taxi, cab	**taxi** (m)	[taksi]
taxi driver	**chauffeur** (m) **de taxi**	[ʃofœr də taksi]
by taxi	**en taxi**	[ã taksi]
taxi stand	**arrêt** (m) **de taxi**	[arɛ də taksi]
to call a taxi	**appeler un taxi**	[aple œ̃ taksi]
to take a taxi	**prendre un taxi**	[prãdr œ̃ taksi]
traffic	**trafic** (m)	[trafik]
traffic jam	**embouteillage** (m)	[ãbutɛjaʒ]
rush hour	**heures** (f pl) **de pointe**	[œr də pwɛ̃t]
to park (vi)	**se garer** (vp)	[sə gare]
to park (vt)	**garer** (vt)	[gare]
parking lot	**parking** (m)	[parkiŋ]
subway	**métro** (m)	[metro]
station	**station** (f)	[stasjõ]
to take the subway	**prendre le métro**	[prãdr lə metro]

| train | train (m) | [trɛ̃] |
| train station | gare (f) | [gar] |

28. City. Life in the city

city, town	ville (f)	[vil]
capital city	capitale (f)	[kapital]
village	village (m)	[vilaʒ]

city map	plan (m) de la ville	[plɑ̃ də la vil]
downtown	centre-ville (m)	[sɑ̃trəvil]
suburb	banlieue (f)	[bɑ̃ljø]
suburban (adj)	de banlieue (adj)	[də bɑ̃ljø]

outskirts	périphérie (f)	[periferi]
environs (suburbs)	alentours (m pl)	[alɑ̃tur]
city block	quartier (m)	[kartje]
residential block (area)	quartier (m) résidentiel	[kartje rezidɑ̃sjɛl]

traffic	trafic (m)	[trafik]
traffic lights	feux (m pl) de circulation	[fø də sirkylasjɔ̃]
public transportation	transport (m) urbain	[trɑ̃spɔr yrbɛ̃]
intersection	carrefour (m)	[karfur]

crosswalk	passage (m) piéton	[pɑsaʒ pjetɔ̃]
pedestrian underpass	passage (m) souterrain	[pɑsaʒ sutɛrɛ̃]
to cross (~ the street)	traverser (vt)	[travɛrse]
pedestrian	piéton (m)	[pjetɔ̃]
sidewalk	trottoir (m)	[trɔtwar]

bridge	pont (m)	[pɔ̃]
embankment (river walk)	quai (m)	[kɛ]
fountain	fontaine (f)	[fɔ̃tɛn]

allée (garden walkway)	allée (f)	[ale]
park	parc (m)	[park]
boulevard	boulevard (m)	[bulvar]
square	place (f)	[plas]
avenue (wide street)	avenue (f)	[avny]
street	rue (f)	[ry]
side street	ruelle (f)	[rɥɛl]
dead end	impasse (f)	[ɛ̃pas]

house	maison (f)	[mɛzɔ̃]
building	édifice (m)	[edifis]
skyscraper	gratte-ciel (m)	[gratsjɛl]

facade	façade (f)	[fasad]
roof	toit (m)	[twa]
window	fenêtre (f)	[fənɛtr]

arch	arc (m)	[ark]
column	colonne (f)	[kɔlɔn]
corner	coin (m)	[kwɛ̃]

store window	vitrine (f)	[vitrin]
signboard (store sign, etc.)	enseigne (f)	[ɑ̃sɛɲ]
poster	affiche (f)	[afiʃ]
advertising poster	affiche (f) publicitaire	[afiʃ pyblisitɛr]
billboard	panneau-réclame (m)	[pano reklam]

garbage, trash	ordures (f pl)	[ɔrdyr]
trashcan (public ~)	poubelle (f)	[pubɛl]
to litter (vi)	jeter ... à terre	[ʒəte ... a tɛr]
garbage dump	décharge (f)	[deʃarʒ]

phone booth	cabine (f) téléphonique	[kabin telefɔnik]
lamppost	réverbère (m)	[revɛrbɛr]
bench (park ~)	banc (m)	[bɑ̃]

police officer	policier (m)	[pɔlisje]
police	police (f)	[pɔlis]
beggar	clochard (m)	[klɔʃar]
homeless (n)	sans-abri (m)	[sɑ̃zabri]

29. Urban institutions

store	magasin (m)	[magazɛ̃]
drugstore, pharmacy	pharmacie (f)	[farmasi]
eyeglass store	opticien (m)	[ɔptisjɛ̃]
shopping mall	centre (m) commercial	[sɑ̃tr kɔmɛrsjal]
supermarket	supermarché (m)	[sypɛrmarʃe]

bakery	boulangerie (f)	[bulɑ̃ʒri]
baker	boulanger (m)	[bulɑ̃ʒe]
candy store	pâtisserie (f)	[pɑtisri]
grocery store	épicerie (f)	[episri]
butcher shop	boucherie (f)	[buʃri]

| produce store | magasin (m) de légumes | [magazɛ̃ də legym] |
| market | marché (m) | [marʃe] |

coffee house	salon (m) de café	[salɔ̃ də kafe]
restaurant	restaurant (m)	[rɛstɔrɑ̃]
pub, bar	brasserie (f)	[brasri]
pizzeria	pizzeria (f)	[pidzerja]

hair salon	salon (m) de coiffure	[salɔ̃ də kwafyr]
post office	poste (f)	[pɔst]
dry cleaners	pressing (m)	[presiŋ]
photo studio	atelier (m) de photo	[atəlje də foto]

shoe store	**magasin** (m) **de chaussures**	[magazɛ̃ də ʃosyr]
bookstore	**librairie** (f)	[librɛri]
sporting goods store	**magasin** (m) **d'articles de sport**	[magazɛ̃ dartikl də spɔr]
clothes repair shop	**atelier** (m) **de retouche**	[atəlje də rətuʃ]
formal wear rental	**location** (f) **de vêtements**	[lɔkasjɔ̃ də vɛtmɑ̃]
video rental store	**location** (f) **de films**	[lɔkasjɔ̃ də film]
circus	**cirque** (m)	[sirk]
zoo	**zoo** (m)	[zoo]
movie theater	**cinéma** (m)	[sinema]
museum	**musée** (m)	[myze]
library	**bibliothèque** (f)	[biblijɔtɛk]
theater	**théâtre** (m)	[teatr]
opera (opera house)	**opéra** (m)	[ɔpera]
nightclub	**boîte** (f) **de nuit**	[bwat də nɥi]
casino	**casino** (m)	[kazino]
mosque	**mosquée** (f)	[mɔske]
synagogue	**synagogue** (f)	[sinagɔg]
cathedral	**cathédrale** (f)	[katedral]
temple	**temple** (m)	[tɑ̃pl]
church	**église** (f)	[egliz]
college	**institut** (m)	[ɛ̃stity]
university	**université** (f)	[ynivɛrsite]
school	**école** (f)	[ekɔl]
prefecture	**préfecture** (f)	[prefɛktyr]
city hall	**mairie** (f)	[meri]
hotel	**hôtel** (m)	[otɛl]
bank	**banque** (f)	[bɑ̃k]
embassy	**ambassade** (f)	[ɑ̃basad]
travel agency	**agence** (f) **de voyages**	[aʒɑ̃s də vwajaʒ]
information office	**bureau** (m) **d'information**	[byro dɛ̃fɔrmasjɔ̃]
currency exchange	**bureau** (m) **de change**	[byro də ʃɑ̃ʒ]
subway	**métro** (m)	[metro]
hospital	**hôpital** (m)	[ɔpital]
gas station	**station-service** (f)	[stasjɔ̃sɛrvis]
parking lot	**parking** (m)	[parkiŋ]

30. Signs

signboard (store sign, etc.)	**enseigne** (f)	[ɑ̃sɛɲ]
notice (door sign, etc.)	**pancarte** (f)	[pɑ̃kart]

poster	**poster** (m)	[pɔstɛr]
direction sign	**indicateur** (m) **de direction**	[ɛ̃dikatœr də dirɛksjɔ̃]
arrow (sign)	**flèche** (f)	[flɛʃ]

caution	**avertissement** (m)	[avɛrtismɑ̃]
warning sign	**panneau** (m) **d'avertissement**	[pano davɛrtismɑ̃]
to warn (vt)	**avertir** (vt)	[avɛrtir]

rest day (weekly ~)	**jour** (m) **de repos**	[ʒur də rəpo]
timetable (schedule)	**horaire** (m)	[ɔrɛr]
opening hours	**heures** (f pl) **d'ouverture**	[zœr duvɛrtyr]

WELCOME!	**BIENVENUE!**	[bjɛ̃vny]
ENTRANCE	**ENTRÉE**	[ɑ̃tre]
EXIT	**SORTIE**	[sɔrti]

PUSH	**POUSSER**	[puse]
PULL	**TIRER**	[tire]
OPEN	**OUVERT**	[uvɛr]
CLOSED	**FERMÉ**	[fɛrme]

| WOMEN | **FEMMES** | [fam] |
| MEN | **HOMMES** | [ɔm] |

DISCOUNTS	**RABAIS**	[sɔld]
SALE	**SOLDES**	[rabɛ]
NEW!	**NOUVEAU!**	[nuvo]
FREE	**GRATUIT**	[gratɥi]

ATTENTION!	**ATTENTION!**	[atɑ̃sjɔ̃]
NO VACANCIES	**COMPLET**	[kɔ̃plɛ]
RESERVED	**RÉSERVÉ**	[rezɛrve]

| ADMINISTRATION | **ADMINISTRATION** | [administrasjɔ̃] |
| STAFF ONLY | **RÉSERVÉ AU PERSONNEL** | [rezɛrve o pɛrsɔnɛl] |

BEWARE OF THE DOG!	**ATTENTION CHIEN MÉCHANT**	[atɑ̃sjɔ̃ ʃjɛ̃ meʃɑ̃]
NO SMOKING	**DÉFENSE DE FUMER**	[defɑ̃s də fyme]
DO NOT TOUCH!	**PRIERE DE NE PAS TOUCHER**	[prijɛr dənəpa tuʃe]

DANGEROUS	**DANGEREUX**	[dɑ̃ʒrø]
DANGER	**DANGER**	[dɑ̃ʒe]
HIGH VOLTAGE	**HAUTE TENSION**	[ot tɑ̃sjɔ̃]
NO SWIMMING!	**BAIGNADE INTERDITE**	[bɛɲad ɛ̃tɛrdit]
OUT OF ORDER	**HORS SERVICE**	[ɔr sɛrvis]
FLAMMABLE	**INFLAMMABLE**	[ɛ̃flamabl]

FORBIDDEN	INTERDIT	[ε̃tεrdi]
NO TRESPASSING!	PASSAGE INTERDIT	[pɑsaʒ ε̃tεrdi]
WET PAINT	PEINTURE FRAÎCHE	[pε̃tyr frεʃ]

31. Shopping

to buy (purchase)	acheter (vt)	[aʃte]
purchase	achat (m)	[aʃa]
to go shopping	faire des achats	[fεr dezaʃa]
shopping	shopping (m)	[ʃɔpiŋ]

| to be open (ab. store) | être ouvert | [εtr uvεr] |
| to be closed | être fermé | [εtr fεrme] |

footwear, shoes	chaussures (f pl)	[ʃosyr]
clothes, clothing	vêtement (m)	[vεtmɑ̃]
cosmetics	produits (m pl) de beauté	[prɔdyi də bote]
food products	produits (m pl) alimentaires	[prɔdyi alimɑ̃tεr]
gift, present	cadeau (m)	[kado]

| salesman | vendeur (m) | [vɑ̃dœr] |
| saleswoman | vendeuse (f) | [vɑ̃døz] |

check out, cash desk	caisse (f)	[kεs]
mirror	miroir (m)	[mirwar]
counter (store ~)	comptoir (m)	[kɔ̃twar]
fitting room	cabine (f) d'essayage	[kabin desεjaʒ]

to try on	essayer (vt)	[eseje]
to fit (ab. dress, etc.)	aller bien	[ale bjε̃]
to like (I like ...)	plaire à ...	[plεr ɑ]

price	prix (m)	[pri]
price tag	étiquette (f) de prix	[etikεt də pri]
to cost (vt)	coûter (vi, vt)	[kute]
How much?	Combien?	[kɔ̃bjε̃]
discount	rabais (m)	[rabε]

inexpensive (adj)	pas cher (adj)	[pɑ ʃεr]
cheap (adj)	bon marché (adj)	[bɔ̃ marʃe]
expensive (adj)	cher (adj)	[ʃεr]
It's expensive	C'est cher	[sε ʃεr]

rental (n)	location (f)	[lɔkasjɔ̃]
to rent (~ a tuxedo)	louer (vt)	[lwe]
credit (trade credit)	crédit (m)	[kredi]
on credit (adv)	à crédit (adv)	[ɑkredi]

CLOTHING & ACCESSORIES

T&P Books Publishing

clothes	**vêtement** (m)	[vɛtmɑ̃]
outerwear	**survêtement** (m)	[syrvɛtmɑ̃]
winter clothing	**vêtement** (m) **d'hiver**	[vɛtmɑ̃ divɛr]

coat (overcoat)	**manteau** (m)	[mɑ̃to]
fur coat	**manteau** (m) **de fourrure**	[mɑ̃to də furyr]
fur jacket	**veste** (f) **en fourrure**	[vɛst ɑ̃ furyr]
down coat	**manteau** (m) **de duvet**	[manto də dyvɛ]

jacket (e.g., leather ~)	**veste** (f)	[vɛst]
raincoat (trenchcoat, etc.)	**imperméable** (m)	[ɛ̃pɛrmeabl]
waterproof (adj)	**imperméable** (adj)	[ɛ̃pɛrmeabl]

shirt (button shirt)	**chemise** (f)	[ʃəmiz]
pants	**pantalon** (m)	[pɑ̃talɔ̃]
jeans	**jean** (m)	[dʒin]
suit jacket	**veston** (m)	[vɛstɔ̃]
suit	**complet** (m)	[kɔ̃plɛ]

dress (frock)	**robe** (f)	[rɔb]
skirt	**jupe** (f)	[ʒyp]
blouse	**chemisette** (f)	[ʃəmizɛt]
knitted jacket (cardigan, etc.)	**veste** (f) **en laine**	[vɛst ɑ̃ lɛn]
jacket (of woman's suit)	**jaquette** (f), **blazer** (m)	[ʒakɛt], [blazɛr]

T-shirt	**tee-shirt** (m)	[tiʃœrt]
shorts (short trousers)	**short** (m)	[ʃɔrt]
tracksuit	**costume** (m) **de sport**	[kɔstym də spɔr]
bathrobe	**peignoir** (m) **de bain**	[pɛɲwar də bɛ̃]
pajamas	**pyjama** (m)	[piʒama]

| sweater | **chandail** (m) | [ʃɑ̃daj] |
| pullover | **pull-over** (m) | [pylovɛr] |

vest	**gilet** (m)	[ʒilɛ]
tailcoat	**queue-de-pie** (f)	[kødpi]
tuxedo	**smoking** (m)	[smɔkiŋ]
uniform	**uniforme** (m)	[ynifɔrm]
workwear	**tenue** (f) **de travail**	[təny də travaj]

| overalls | salopette (f) | [salɔpɛt] |
| coat (e.g., doctor's smock) | blouse (f) | [bluz] |

34. Clothing. Underwear

underwear	sous-vêtements (m pl)	[suvɛtmɑ̃]
boxers	boxer (m)	[bɔksɛr]
panties	slip (m) de femme	[slip də fam]
undershirt (A-shirt)	maillot (m) de corps	[majo də kɔr]
socks	chaussettes (f pl)	[ʃosɛt]

nightgown	chemise (f) de nuit	[ʃəmiz də nɥi]
bra	soutien-gorge (m)	[sutjɛ̃gɔrʒ]
knee highs (knee-high socks)	chaussettes (f pl) hautes	[ʃosɛt ot]
pantyhose	collants (m pl)	[kɔlɑ̃]
stockings (thigh highs)	bas (m pl)	[ba]
bathing suit	maillot (m) de bain	[majo də bɛ̃]

35. Headwear

hat	chapeau (m)	[ʃapo]
fedora	chapeau (m) feutre	[ʃapo føtr]
baseball cap	casquette (f) de base-ball	[kaskɛt də bɛzbol]
flatcap	casquette (f)	[kaskɛt]

beret	béret (m)	[berɛ]
hood	capuche (f)	[kapyʃ]
panama hat	panama (m)	[panama]
knit cap (knitted hat)	bonnet (m) de laine	[bɔnɛ də lɛn]

| headscarf | foulard (m) | [fular] |
| women's hat | chapeau (m) de femme | [ʃapo də fam] |

hard hat	casque (m)	[kask]
garrison cap	calot (m)	[kalo]
helmet	casque (m)	[kask]

| derby | melon (m) | [məlɔ̃] |
| top hat | haut-de-forme (m) | [o də fɔrm] |

36. Footwear

footwear	chaussures (f pl)	[ʃosyr]
shoes (men's shoes)	bottines (f pl)	[bɔtin]
shoes (women's shoes)	souliers (m pl)	[sulje]

boots (cowboy ~)	**bottes** (f pl)	[bɔt]
slippers	**chaussons** (m pl)	[ʃosɔ̃]
tennis shoes (e.g., Nike ~)	**tennis** (m pl)	[tenis]
sneakers	**baskets** (f pl)	[baskɛt]
(e.g., Converse ~)		
sandals	**sandales** (f pl)	[sɑ̃dal]
cobbler (shoe repairer)	**cordonnier** (m)	[kɔrdɔnje]
heel	**talon** (m)	[talɔ̃]
pair (of shoes)	**paire** (f)	[pɛr]
shoestring	**lacet** (m)	[lase]
to lace (vt)	**lacer** (vt)	[lase]
shoehorn	**chausse-pied** (m)	[ʃospje]
shoe polish	**cirage** (m)	[siraʒ]

37. Personal accessories

gloves	**gants** (m pl)	[gɑ̃]
mittens	**moufles** (f pl)	[mufl]
scarf (muffler)	**écharpe** (f)	[eʃarp]
glasses (eyeglasses)	**lunettes** (f pl)	[lynɛt]
frame (eyeglass ~)	**monture** (f)	[mɔ̃tyr]
umbrella	**parapluie** (m)	[paraplɥi]
walking stick	**canne** (f)	[kan]
hairbrush	**brosse** (f) **à cheveux**	[brɔs ɑ ʃəvø]
fan	**éventail** (m)	[evɑ̃taj]
tie (necktie)	**cravate** (f)	[kravat]
bow tie	**nœud papillon** (m)	[nø papijɔ̃]
suspenders	**bretelles** (f pl)	[brətɛl]
handkerchief	**mouchoir** (m)	[muʃwar]
comb	**peigne** (m)	[pɛɲ]
barrette	**barrette** (f)	[barɛt]
hairpin	**épingle** (f) **à cheveux**	[epɛ̃gl ɑ ʃəvø]
buckle	**boucle** (f)	[bukl]
belt	**ceinture** (f)	[sɛ̃tyr]
shoulder strap	**bandoulière** (f)	[bɑ̃duljɛr]
bag (handbag)	**sac** (m)	[sak]
purse	**sac** (m) **à main**	[sak ɑ mɛ̃]
backpack	**sac** (m) **à dos**	[sak ɑ do]

38. Clothing. Miscellaneous

fashion	mode (f)	[mɔd]
in vogue (adj)	à la mode (adj)	[alamɔd]
fashion designer	couturier (m), créateur (m) de mode	[kutyrje], [kreatœr də mɔd]

collar	col (m)	[kɔl]
pocket	poche (f)	[pɔʃ]
pocket (as adj)	de poche (adj)	[də pɔʃ]
sleeve	manche (f)	[mãʃ]
hanging loop	bride (f)	[brid]
fly (on trousers)	braguette (f)	[bragɛt]

zipper (fastener)	fermeture (f) à glissière	[fɛrmətyr a glisjɛr]
fastener	agrafe (f)	[agraf]
button	bouton (m)	[butõ]
buttonhole	boutonnière (f)	[butɔnjɛr]
to come off (ab. button)	sauter (vi)	[sote]

to sew (vi, vt)	coudre (vi, vt)	[kudr]
to embroider (vi, vt)	broder (vt)	[brɔde]
embroidery	broderie (f)	[brɔdri]
sewing needle	aiguille (f)	[eguij]
thread	fil (m)	[fil]
seam	couture (f)	[kutyr]

to get dirty (vi)	se salir (vp)	[sə salir]
stain (mark, spot)	tache (f)	[taʃ]
to crease, crumple (vi)	se froisser (vp)	[sə frwase]
to tear, to rip (vt)	déchirer (vt)	[deʃire]
clothes moth	mite (f)	[mit]

39. Personal care. Cosmetics

toothpaste	dentifrice (m)	[dãtifris]
toothbrush	brosse (f) à dents	[brɔs a dã]
to brush one's teeth	se brosser les dents	[sə brɔse le dã]

razor	rasoir (m)	[razwar]
shaving cream	crème (f) à raser	[krɛm a raze]
to shave (vi)	se raser (vp)	[sə raze]

soap	savon (m)	[savõ]
shampoo	shampooing (m)	[ʃãpwɛ̃]

scissors	ciseaux (m pl)	[sizo]
nail file	lime (f) à ongles	[lim a õgl]
nail clippers	pinces (f pl) à ongles	[pɛ̃s a õgl]

tweezers	**pince** (f)	[pɛ̃s]
cosmetics	**cosmétiques** (m pl)	[kɔsmetik]
face mask	**masque** (m) **de beauté**	[mask də bote]
manicure	**manucure** (f)	[manykyr]
to have a manicure	**se faire les ongles**	[sə fɛr le zɔ̃gl]
pedicure	**pédicurie** (f)	[pedikyri]
make-up bag	**trousse** (f) **de toilette**	[trus də twalɛt]
face powder	**poudre** (f)	[pudr]
powder compact	**poudrier** (m)	[pudrije]
blusher	**fard** (m) **à joues**	[far a ʒu]
perfume (bottled)	**parfum** (m)	[parfœ̃]
toilet water (perfume)	**eau** (f) **de toilette**	[o də twalɛt]
lotion	**lotion** (f)	[losjɔ̃]
cologne	**eau de Cologne** (f)	[o də kɔlɔɲ]
eyeshadow	**fard** (m) **à paupières**	[far a popjɛr]
eyeliner	**crayon** (m) **à paupières**	[krɛjɔ̃ a popjɛr]
mascara	**mascara** (m)	[maskara]
lipstick	**rouge** (m) **à lèvres**	[ruʒ a lɛvr]
nail polish, enamel	**vernis** (m) **à ongles**	[vɛrni a ɔ̃gl]
hair spray	**laque** (f) **pour les cheveux**	[lak pur le ʃəvø]
deodorant	**déodorant** (m)	[deɔdɔrɑ̃]
cream	**crème** (f)	[krɛm]
face cream	**crème** (f) **pour le visage**	[krɛm pur lə vizaʒ]
hand cream	**crème** (f) **pour les mains**	[krɛm pur le mɛ̃]
anti-wrinkle cream	**crème** (f) **anti-rides**	[krɛm ɑ̃tirid]
day cream	**crème** (f) **de jour**	[krɛm də ʒur]
night cream	**crème** (f) **de nuit**	[krɛm də nɥi]
day (as adj)	**de jour** (adj)	[də ʒur]
night (as adj)	**de nuit** (adj)	[də nɥi]
tampon	**tampon** (m)	[tɑ̃pɔ̃]
toilet paper	**papier** (m) **de toilette**	[papje də twalɛt]
hair dryer	**sèche-cheveux** (m)	[sɛʃʃəvø]

40. Watches. Clocks

watch (wristwatch)	**montre** (f)	[mɔ̃tr]
dial	**cadran** (m)	[kadrɑ̃]
hand (of clock, watch)	**aiguille** (f)	[egɥij]
metal watch band	**bracelet** (m)	[braslɛ]
watch strap	**bracelet** (m)	[braslɛ]
battery	**pile** (f)	[pil]
to be dead (battery)	**être déchargé**	[ɛtr deʃarʒe]

to change a battery	changer de pile	[ʃɑ̃ʒe də pil]
to run fast	avancer (vi)	[avɑ̃se]
to run slow	retarder (vi)	[rətarde]

wall clock	pendule (f)	[pɑ̃dyl]
hourglass	sablier (m)	[sablije]
sundial	cadran (m) solaire	[kadrɑ̃ sɔlɛr]
alarm clock	réveil (m)	[revɛj]
watchmaker	horloger (m)	[ɔrlɔʒe]
to repair (vt)	réparer (vt)	[repare]

EVERYDAY EXPERIENCE

T&P Books Publishing

41. Money

money	**argent** (m)	[arʒɑ̃]
currency exchange	**échange** (m)	[eʃɑ̃ʒ]
exchange rate	**cours** (m) **de change**	[kur də ʃɑ̃ʒ]
ATM	**distributeur** (m)	[distribytœr]
coin	**monnaie** (f)	[mɔnɛ]

| dollar | **dollar** (m) | [dɔlar] |
| euro | **euro** (m) | [øro] |

lira	**lire** (f)	[lir]
Deutschmark	**mark** (m) **allemand**	[mark almɑ̃]
franc	**franc** (m)	[frɑ̃]
pound sterling	**livre sterling** (f)	[livr stɛrliŋ]
yen	**yen** (m)	[jɛn]

debt	**dette** (f)	[dɛt]
debtor	**débiteur** (m)	[debitœr]
to lend (money)	**prêter** (vt)	[prete]
to borrow (vi, vt)	**emprunter** (vt)	[ɑ̃prœ̃te]

bank	**banque** (f)	[bɑ̃k]
account	**compte** (m)	[kɔ̃t]
to deposit (vt)	**verser** (vt)	[vɛrse]
to deposit into the account	**verser dans le compte**	[vɛrse dɑ̃ lə kɔ̃t]
to withdraw (vt)	**retirer du compte**	[rətire dy kɔ̃t]

credit card	**carte** (f) **de crédit**	[kart də kredi]
cash	**espèces** (f pl)	[ɛspɛs]
check	**chèque** (m)	[ʃɛk]
to write a check	**faire un chèque**	[fɛr œ̃ ʃɛk]
checkbook	**chéquier** (m)	[ʃekje]

wallet	**portefeuille** (m)	[pɔrtəfœj]
change purse	**bourse** (f)	[burs]
billfold	**porte-monnaie** (m)	[pɔrtmɔnɛ]
safe	**coffre fort** (m)	[kɔfr fɔr]

heir	**héritier** (m)	[eritje]
inheritance	**héritage** (m)	[eritaʒ]
fortune (wealth)	**fortune** (f)	[fɔrtyn]

lease	**location** (f)	[lɔkasjɔ̃]
rent (money)	**loyer** (m)	[lwaje]
to rent (sth from sb)	**louer** (vt)	[lwe]

price	**prix** (m)	[pri]
cost	**coût** (m)	[ku]
sum	**somme** (f)	[sɔm]

to spend (vt)	**dépenser** (vt)	[depãse]
expenses	**dépenses** (f pl)	[depãs]
to economize (vi, vt)	**économiser** (vt)	[ekɔnɔmize]
economical	**économe** (adj)	[ekɔnɔm]

to pay (vi, vt)	**payer** (vi, vt)	[peje]
payment	**paiement** (m)	[pɛmã]
change (give the ~)	**monnaie** (f)	[mɔnɛ]

tax	**impôt** (m)	[ɛ̃po]
fine	**amende** (f)	[amãd]
to fine (vt)	**mettre une amende**	[mɛtr ynamãd]

42. Post. Postal service

post office	**poste** (f)	[pɔst]
mail (letters, etc.)	**courrier** (m)	[kurje]
mailman	**facteur** (m)	[faktœr]
opening hours	**heures** (f pl) **d'ouverture**	[zœr duvɛrtyr]

letter	**lettre** (f)	[lɛtr]
registered letter	**recommandé** (m)	[rəkɔmãde]
postcard	**carte** (f) **postale**	[kart pɔstal]
telegram	**télégramme** (m)	[telegram]
package (parcel)	**colis** (m)	[kɔli]
money transfer	**mandat** (m) **postal**	[mãda pɔstal]

to receive (vt)	**recevoir** (vt)	[rəsəvwar]
to send (vt)	**envoyer** (vt)	[ãvwaje]
sending	**envoi** (m)	[ãvwa]

address	**adresse** (f)	[adrɛs]
ZIP code	**code** (m) **postal**	[kɔd pɔstal]
sender	**expéditeur** (m)	[ɛkspeditœr]
receiver	**destinataire** (m)	[dɛstinatɛr]

| name (first name) | **prénom** (m) | [prenɔ̃] |
| surname (last name) | **nom** (m) **de famille** | [nɔ̃ də famij] |

postage rate	**tarif** (m)	[tarif]
standard (adj)	**normal** (adj)	[nɔrmal]
economical (adj)	**économique** (adj)	[ekɔnɔmik]

weight	**poids** (m)	[pwa]
to weigh (~ letters)	**peser** (vt)	[pəze]
envelope	**enveloppe** (f)	[ãvlɔp]

| postage stamp | timbre (m) | [tɛ̃br] |
| to stamp an envelope | timbrer (vt) | [tɛ̃bre] |

43. Banking

| bank | banque (f) | [bɑ̃k] |
| branch (of bank, etc.) | agence (f) bancaire | [aʒɑ̃s bɑ̃kɛr] |

| bank clerk, consultant | conseiller (m) | [kɔ̃seje] |
| manager (director) | gérant (m) | [ʒerɑ̃] |

bank account	compte (m)	[kɔ̃t]
account number	numéro (m) du compte	[nymero dy kɔ̃t]
checking account	compte (m) courant	[kɔ̃t kurɑ̃]
savings account	compte (m) sur livret	[kɔ̃t syr livrɛ]

| to open an account | ouvrir un compte | [uvrir œ̃ kɔ̃t] |
| to close the account | clôturer le compte | [klotyre lə kɔ̃t] |

| to deposit into the account | verser dans le compte | [vɛrse dɑ̃ lə kɔ̃t] |
| to withdraw (vt) | retirer du compte | [rətire dy kɔ̃t] |

| deposit | dépôt (m) | [depo] |
| to make a deposit | faire un dépôt | [fɛr œ̃ depo] |

| wire transfer | virement (m) bancaire | [virmɑ̃ bɑ̃kɛr] |
| to wire, to transfer | faire un transfert | [fɛr œ̃ trɑ̃sfɛr] |

| sum | somme (f) | [sɔm] |
| How much? | Combien? | [kɔ̃bjɛ̃] |

| signature | signature (f) | [siɲatyr] |
| to sign (vt) | signer (vt) | [siɲe] |

| credit card | carte (f) de crédit | [kart də kredi] |
| code (PIN code) | code (m) | [kɔd] |

| credit card number | numéro (m) de carte de crédit | [nymero də kart də kredi] |
| ATM | distributeur (m) | [distribytœr] |

check	chèque (m)	[ʃɛk]
to write a check	faire un chèque	[fɛr œ̃ ʃɛk]
checkbook	chéquier (m)	[ʃekje]

loan (bank ~)	crédit (m)	[kredi]
to apply for a loan	demander un crédit	[dəmɑ̃de œ̃ kredi]
to get a loan	prendre un crédit	[prɑ̃dr œ̃ kredi]
to give a loan	accorder un crédit	[akɔrde œ̃ kredi]
guarantee	gage (m)	[gaʒ]

44. Telephone. Phone conversation

telephone	**téléphone** (m)	[telefɔn]
mobile phone	**portable** (m)	[pɔrtabl]
answering machine	**répondeur** (m)	[repɔ̃dœr]
to call (by phone)	**téléphoner, appeler**	[telefɔne], [aple]
phone call	**appel** (m)	[apɛl]
to dial a number	**composer le numéro**	[kɔ̃poze lə nymero]
Hello!	**Allô!**	[alo]
to ask (vt)	**demander** (vt)	[dəmɑ̃de]
to answer (vi, vt)	**répondre** (vi, vt)	[repɔ̃dr]
to hear (vt)	**entendre** (vt)	[ɑ̃tɑ̃dr]
well (adv)	**bien** (adv)	[bjɛ̃]
not well (adv)	**mal** (adv)	[mal]
noises (interference)	**bruits** (m pl)	[brɥi]
receiver	**récepteur** (m)	[resɛptœr]
to pick up (~ the phone)	**décrocher** (vt)	[dekrɔʃe]
to hang up (~ the phone)	**raccrocher** (vi)	[rakrɔʃe]
busy (adj)	**occupé** (adj)	[ɔkype]
to ring (ab. phone)	**sonner** (vi)	[sɔ̃]
telephone book	**carnet** (m) **de téléphone**	[karnɛ də telefɔn]
local (adj)	**local** (adj)	[lɔkal]
local call	**appel** (m) **local**	[apɛl lɔkal]
long distance (~ call)	**interurbain** (adj)	[ɛ̃tɛryrbɛ̃]
long-distance call	**appel** (m) **interurbain**	[apɛl ɛ̃tɛryrbɛ̃]
international (adj)	**international** (adj)	[ɛ̃tɛrnasjɔnal]
international call	**appel** (m) **international**	[apɛl ɛ̃tɛrnasjɔnal]

45. Mobile telephone

mobile phone	**portable** (m)	[pɔrtabl]
display	**écran** (m)	[ekrɑ̃]
button	**bouton** (m)	[butɔ̃]
SIM card	**carte SIM** (f)	[kart sim]
battery	**pile** (f)	[pil]
to be dead (battery)	**être déchargé**	[ɛtr deʃarʒe]
charger	**chargeur** (m)	[ʃarʒœr]
menu	**menu** (m)	[məny]
settings	**réglages** (m pl)	[reglaʒ]
tune (melody)	**mélodie** (f)	[melɔdi]
to select (vt)	**sélectionner** (vt)	[selɛksjɔne]

calculator	calculatrice (f)	[kalkylatris]
voice mail	répondeur (m)	[repɔ̃dœr]
alarm clock	réveil (m)	[revɛj]
contacts	contacts (m pl)	[kɔ̃takt]

| SMS (text message) | SMS (m) | [esemes] |
| subscriber | abonné (m) | [abɔne] |

46. Stationery

| ballpoint pen | stylo (m) à bille | [stilo α bij] |
| fountain pen | stylo (m) à plume | [stilo α plym] |

pencil	crayon (m)	[krɛjɔ̃]
highlighter	marqueur (m)	[markœr]
felt-tip pen	feutre (m)	[føtr]

| notepad | bloc-notes (m) | [blɔknɔt] |
| agenda (diary) | agenda (m) | [aʒɛ̃da] |

ruler	règle (f)	[rɛgl]
calculator	calculatrice (f)	[kalkylatris]
eraser	gomme (f)	[gɔm]
thumbtack	punaise (f)	[pynɛz]
paper clip	trombone (m)	[trɔ̃bɔn]

glue	colle (f)	[kɔl]
stapler	agrafeuse (f)	[agraføz]
hole punch	perforateur (m)	[pɛrfɔratœr]
pencil sharpener	taille-crayon (m)	[tajkrɛjɔ̃]

47. Foreign languages

language	langue (f)	[lɑ̃g]
foreign language	langue (f) étrangère	[lɑ̃g etrɑ̃ʒɛr]
to study (vt)	étudier (vt)	[etydje]
to learn (language, etc.)	apprendre (vt)	[aprɑ̃dr]

to read (vi, vt)	lire (vi, vt)	[lir]
to speak (vi, vt)	parler (vi)	[parle]
to understand (vt)	comprendre (vt)	[kɔ̃prɑ̃dr]
to write (vt)	écrire (vt)	[ekrir]

fast (adv)	vite (adv)	[vit]
slowly (adv)	lentement (adv)	[lɑ̃tmɑ̃]
fluently (adv)	couramment (adv)	[kuramɑ̃]
rules	règles (f pl)	[rɛgl]
grammar	grammaire (f)	[gramɛr]

| vocabulary | vocabulaire (m) | [vɔkabylɛr] |
| phonetics | phonétique (f) | [fɔnetik] |

textbook	manuel (m)	[manɥɛl]
dictionary	dictionnaire (m)	[diksjɔnɛr]
teach-yourself book	manuel (m) autodidacte	[manɥɛl otodidakt]
phrasebook	guide (m) de conversation	[gid də kɔ̃vɛrsasjɔ̃]

cassette	cassette (f)	[kasɛt]
videotape	cassette (f) vidéo	[kasɛt video]
CD, compact disc	CD (m)	[sede]
DVD	DVD (m)	[devede]

alphabet	alphabet (m)	[alfabɛ]
to spell (vt)	épeler (vt)	[eple]
pronunciation	prononciation (f)	[prɔnɔ̃sjasjɔ̃]

accent	accent (m)	[aksɑ̃]
with an accent	avec un accent	[avɛk œn aksɑ̃]
without an accent	sans accent	[sɑ̃ zaksɑ̃]

| word | mot (m) | [mo] |
| meaning | sens (m) | [sɑ̃s] |

course (e.g., a French ~)	cours (m pl)	[kur]
to sign up	s'inscrire (vp)	[sɛ̃skrir]
teacher	professeur (m)	[prɔfɛsœr]

translation (process)	traduction (f)	[tradyksjɔ̃]
translation (text, etc.)	traduction (f)	[tradyksjɔ̃]
translator	traducteur (m)	[tradyktœr]
interpreter	interprète (m)	[ɛ̃tɛrprɛt]

| polyglot | polyglotte (m) | [pɔliglɔt] |
| memory | mémoire (f) | [memwar] |

T&P BOOKS

MEALS. RESTAURANT

T&P Books Publishing

48. Table setting

spoon	**cuillère** (f)	[kɥijɛr]
knife	**couteau** (m)	[kuto]
fork	**fourchette** (f)	[furʃɛt]
cup (e.g., coffee ~)	**tasse** (f)	[tɑs]
plate (dinner ~)	**assiette** (f)	[asjɛt]
saucer	**soucoupe** (f)	[sukup]
napkin (on table)	**serviette** (f)	[sɛrvjɛt]
toothpick	**cure-dent** (m)	[kyrdɑ̃]

49. Restaurant

restaurant	**restaurant** (m)	[rɛstɔrɑ̃]
coffee house	**salon** (m) **de café**	[salɔ̃ də kafe]
pub, bar	**bar** (m)	[bar]
tearoom	**salon** (m) **de thé**	[salɔ̃ də te]
waiter	**serveur** (m)	[sɛrvœr]
waitress	**serveuse** (f)	[sɛrvøz]
bartender	**barman** (m)	[barman]
menu	**carte** (f)	[kart]
wine list	**carte** (f) **des vins**	[kart de vɛ̃]
to book a table	**réserver une table**	[rezɛrve yn tabl]
course, dish	**plat** (m)	[pla]
to order (meal)	**commander** (vt)	[kɔmɑ̃de]
to make an order	**faire la commande**	[fɛr la kɔmɑ̃d]
aperitif	**apéritif** (m)	[aperitif]
appetizer	**hors-d'œuvre** (m)	[ɔrdœvr]
dessert	**dessert** (m)	[desɛr]
check	**addition** (f)	[adisjɔ̃]
to pay the check	**régler l'addition**	[regle ladisjɔ̃]
to give change	**rendre la monnaie**	[rɑ̃dr la mɔnɛ]
tip	**pourboire** (m)	[purbwar]

50. Meals

food	**nourriture** (f)	[nurityr]
to eat (vi, vt)	**manger** (vi, vt)	[mɑ̃ʒe]

breakfast	petit déjeuner (m)	[pəti deʒœne]
to have breakfast	prendre le petit déjeuner	[prãdr ləpti deʒœne]
lunch	déjeuner (m)	[deʒœne]
to have lunch	déjeuner (vi)	[deʒœne]
dinner	dîner (m)	[dine]
to have dinner	dîner (vi)	[dine]

| appetite | appétit (m) | [apeti] |
| Enjoy your meal! | Bon appétit! | [bɔn apeti] |

to open (~ a bottle)	ouvrir (vt)	[uvrir]
to spill (liquid)	renverser (vt)	[rãvɛrse]
to spill out (vi)	se renverser (vp)	[sə rãvɛrse]

to boil (vi)	bouillir (vi)	[bujir]
to boil (vt)	faire bouillir	[fɛr bujir]
boiled (~ water)	bouilli (adj)	[buji]
to chill, cool down (vt)	refroidir (vt)	[rəfrwadir]
to chill (vi)	se refroidir (vp)	[sə rəfrwadir]

| taste, flavor | goût (m) | [gu] |
| aftertaste | arrière-goût (m) | [arjɛrgu] |

to slim down (lose weight)	suivre un régime	[sɥivr œ̃ reʒim]
diet	régime (m)	[reʒim]
vitamin	vitamine (f)	[vitamin]
calorie	calorie (f)	[kalɔri]
vegetarian (n)	végétarien (m)	[veʒetarjɛ̃]
vegetarian (adj)	végétarien (adj)	[veʒetarjɛ̃]

fats (nutrient)	lipides (m pl)	[lipid]
proteins	protéines (f pl)	[prɔtein]
carbohydrates	glucides (m pl)	[glysid]
slice (of lemon, ham)	tranche (f)	[trãʃ]
piece (of cake, pie)	morceau (m)	[mɔrso]
crumb (of bread, cake, etc.)	miette (f)	[mjɛt]

51. Cooked dishes

course, dish	plat (m)	[pla]
cuisine	cuisine (f)	[kɥizin]
recipe	recette (f)	[rəsɛt]
portion	portion (f)	[pɔrsjɔ̃]

| salad | salade (f) | [salad] |
| soup | soupe (f) | [sup] |

| clear soup (broth) | bouillon (m) | [bujɔ̃] |
| sandwich (bread) | sandwich (m) | [sãdwitʃ] |

fried eggs	les œufs brouillés	[lezø bruje]
fried meatballs	boulette (f)	[bulɛt]
hamburger (beefburger)	hamburger (m)	[ãbœrgœr]
beefsteak	steak (m)	[stɛk]
stew	rôti (m)	[roti]

side dish	garniture (f)	[garnityr]
spaghetti	spaghettis (m pl)	[spagɛti]
mashed potatoes	purée (f)	[pyre]
pizza	pizza (f)	[pidza]
porridge (oatmeal, etc.)	bouillie (f)	[buji]
omelet	omelette (f)	[ɔmlɛt]

boiled (e.g., ~ beef)	cuit à l'eau (adj)	[kɥitɑlo]
smoked (adj)	fumé (adj)	[fyme]
fried (adj)	frit (adj)	[fri]
dried (adj)	sec (adj)	[sɛk]
frozen (adj)	congelé (adj)	[kɔ̃ʒle]
pickled (adj)	mariné (adj)	[marine]

sweet (sugary)	sucré (adj)	[sykre]
salty (adj)	salé (adj)	[sale]
cold (adj)	froid (adj)	[frwa]
hot (adj)	chaud (adj)	[ʃo]
bitter (adj)	amer (adj)	[amɛr]
tasty (adj)	bon (adj)	[bɔ̃]

to cook in boiling water	cuire à l'eau	[kɥir a lo]
to cook (dinner)	préparer (vt)	[prepare]
to fry (vt)	faire frire	[fɛr frir]
to heat up (food)	réchauffer (vt)	[reʃofe]

to salt (vt)	saler (vt)	[sale]
to pepper (vt)	poivrer (vt)	[pwavre]
to grate (vt)	râper (vt)	[rɑpe]
peel (n)	peau (f)	[po]
to peel (vt)	éplucher (vt)	[eplyʃe]

52. Food

meat	viande (f)	[vjɑ̃d]
chicken	poulet (m)	[pulɛ]
Rock Cornish hen (poussin)	poulet (m)	[pulɛ]
duck	canard (m)	[kanar]
goose	oie (f)	[wa]
game	gibier (m)	[ʒibje]
turkey	dinde (f)	[dɛ̃d]
pork	du porc	[dy pɔr]
veal	du veau	[dy vo]

lamb	**du mouton**	[dy mutɔ̃]
beef	**du bœuf**	[dy bœf]
rabbit	**lapin** (m)	[lapɛ̃]

sausage (bologna, pepperoni, etc.)	**saucisson** (m)	[sosisɔ̃]
vienna sausage (frankfurter)	**saucisse** (f)	[sosis]
bacon	**bacon** (m)	[bekɔn]
ham	**jambon** (m)	[ʒɑ̃bɔ̃]
gammon	**cuisse** (f)	[kɥis]

pâté	**pâté** (m)	[pɑte]
liver	**foie** (m)	[fwa]
lard	**lard** (m)	[lar]
hamburger (ground beef)	**farce** (f)	[fars]
tongue	**langue** (f)	[lɑ̃g]

egg	**œuf** (m)	[œf]
eggs	**les œufs**	[lezø]
egg white	**blanc** (m) **d'œuf**	[blɑ̃ dœf]
egg yolk	**jaune** (m) **d'œuf**	[ʒon dœf]

fish	**poisson** (m)	[pwasɔ̃]
seafood	**fruits** (m pl) **de mer**	[frɥi də mɛr]
crustaceans	**crustacés** (m pl)	[krystase]
caviar	**caviar** (m)	[kavjar]

crab	**crabe** (m)	[krab]
shrimp	**crevette** (f)	[krəvɛt]
oyster	**huître** (f)	[ɥitr]
spiny lobster	**langoustine** (f)	[lɑ̃gustin]
octopus	**poulpe** (m)	[pulp]
squid	**calamar** (m)	[kalamar]

sturgeon	**esturgeon** (m)	[ɛstyrʒɔ̃]
salmon	**saumon** (m)	[somɔ̃]
halibut	**flétan** (m)	[fletɑ̃]

cod	**morue** (f)	[mɔry]
mackerel	**maquereau** (m)	[makro]
tuna	**thon** (m)	[tɔ̃]
eel	**anguille** (f)	[ɑ̃gij]

trout	**truite** (f)	[trɥit]
sardine	**sardine** (f)	[sardin]
pike	**brochet** (m)	[brɔʃɛ]
herring	**hareng** (m)	[arɑ̃]

bread	**pain** (m)	[pɛ̃]
cheese	**fromage** (m)	[frɔmaʒ]
sugar	**sucre** (m)	[sykr]

salt	**sel** (m)	[sɛl]
rice	**riz** (m)	[ri]
pasta	**pâtes** (m pl)	[pɑt]
noodles	**nouilles** (f pl)	[nuj]
butter	**beurre** (m)	[bœr]
vegetable oil	**huile** (f) **végétale**	[ɥil veʒetal]
sunflower oil	**huile** (f) **de tournesol**	[ɥil də turnəsɔl]
margarine	**margarine** (f)	[margarin]
olives	**olives** (f pl)	[ɔliv]
olive oil	**huile** (f) **d'olive**	[ɥil dɔliv]
milk	**lait** (m)	[lɛ]
condensed milk	**lait** (m) **condensé**	[lɛ kõdɑ̃se]
yogurt	**yogourt** (m)	[jaurt]
sour cream	**crème** (f) **aigre**	[krɛm ɛgr]
cream (of milk)	**crème** (f)	[krɛm]
mayonnaise	**sauce** (f) **mayonnaise**	[sos majɔnɛz]
buttercream	**crème** (f) **au beurre**	[krɛm o bœr]
cereal grains (wheat, etc.)	**gruau** (m)	[gryo]
flour	**farine** (f)	[farin]
canned food	**conserves** (f pl)	[kõsɛrv]
cornflakes	**pétales** (m pl) **de maïs**	[petal də mais]
honey	**miel** (m)	[mjɛl]
jam	**confiture** (f)	[kõfityr]
chewing gum	**gomme** (f) **à mâcher**	[gɔm a mɑʃe]

53. Drinks

water	**eau** (f)	[o]
drinking water	**eau** (f) **potable**	[o pɔtabl]
mineral water	**eau** (f) **minérale**	[o mineral]
still (adj)	**plate** (adj)	[plat]
carbonated (adj)	**gazeuse** (adj)	[gazøz]
sparkling (adj)	**pétillante** (adj)	[petijɑ̃t]
ice	**glace** (f)	[glas]
with ice	**avec de la glace**	[avɛk dəla glas]
non-alcoholic (adj)	**sans alcool**	[sã zalkɔl]
soft drink	**boisson** (f) **non alcoolisée**	[bwasõ nonalkɔlize]
refreshing drink	**rafraîchissement** (m)	[rafrɛʃismã]
lemonade	**limonade** (f)	[limɔnad]
liquors	**boissons** (f pl) **alcoolisées**	[bwasõ alkɔlize]

wine	vin (m)	[vɛ̃]
white wine	vin (m) blanc	[vɛ̃ blɑ̃]
red wine	vin (m) rouge	[vɛ̃ ruʒ]

liqueur	liqueur (f)	[likœr]
champagne	champagne (m)	[ʃɑ̃paɲ]
vermouth	vermouth (m)	[vɛrmut]

whisky	whisky (m)	[wiski]
vodka	vodka (f)	[vɔdka]
gin	gin (m)	[dʒin]
cognac	cognac (m)	[kɔɲak]
rum	rhum (m)	[rɔm]

coffee	café (m)	[kafe]
black coffee	café (m) noir	[kafe nwar]
coffee with milk	café (m) au lait	[kafe o lɛ]
cappuccino	cappuccino (m)	[kaputʃino]
instant coffee	café (m) soluble	[kafe sɔlybl]

milk	lait (m)	[lɛ]
cocktail	cocktail (m)	[kɔktɛl]
milkshake	cocktail (m) au lait	[kɔktɛl o lɛ]

juice	jus (m)	[ʒy]
tomato juice	jus (m) de tomate	[ʒy də tɔmat]
orange juice	jus (m) d'orange	[ʒy dɔrɑ̃ʒ]
freshly squeezed juice	jus (m) pressé	[ʒy prese]

beer	bière (f)	[bjɛr]
light beer	bière (f) blonde	[bjɛr blɔ̃d]
dark beer	bière (f) brune	[bjɛr bryn]

tea	thé (m)	[te]
black tea	thé (m) noir	[te nwar]
green tea	thé (m) vert	[te vɛr]

54. Vegetables

| vegetables | légumes (m pl) | [legym] |
| greens | verdure (f) | [vɛrdyr] |

tomato	tomate (f)	[tɔmat]
cucumber	concombre (m)	[kɔ̃kɔ̃br]
carrot	carotte (f)	[karɔt]
potato	pomme (f) de terre	[pɔm də tɛr]
onion	oignon (m)	[ɔɲɔ̃]
garlic	ail (m)	[aj]
cabbage	chou (m)	[ʃu]
cauliflower	chou-fleur (m)	[ʃuflœr]

Brussels sprouts	**chou** (m) **de Bruxelles**	[ʃu də brysɛl]
broccoli	**brocoli** (m)	[brɔkɔli]

beetroot	**betterave** (f)	[bɛtrav]
eggplant	**aubergine** (f)	[obɛrʒin]
zucchini	**courgette** (f)	[kurʒɛt]
pumpkin	**potiron** (m)	[pɔtirɔ̃]
turnip	**navet** (m)	[navɛ]

parsley	**persil** (m)	[pɛrsi]
dill	**fenouil** (m)	[fənuj]
lettuce	**laitue** (f), **salade** (f)	[lety], [salad]
celery	**céleri** (m)	[sɛlri]
asparagus	**asperge** (f)	[aspɛrʒ]
spinach	**épinard** (m)	[epinar]

pea	**pois** (m)	[pwa]
beans	**fèves** (f pl)	[fɛv]
corn (maize)	**maïs** (m)	[mais]
kidney bean	**haricot** (m)	[ariko]

bell pepper	**poivron** (m)	[pwavrɔ̃]
radish	**radis** (m)	[radi]
artichoke	**artichaut** (m)	[artiʃo]

55. Fruits. Nuts

fruit	**fruit** (m)	[frɥi]
apple	**pomme** (f)	[pɔm]
pear	**poire** (f)	[pwar]
lemon	**citron** (m)	[sitrɔ̃]
orange	**orange** (f)	[ɔrɑ̃ʒ]
strawberry	**fraise** (f)	[frɛz]

mandarin	**mandarine** (f)	[mɑ̃darin]
plum	**prune** (f)	[pryn]
peach	**pêche** (f)	[pɛʃ]
apricot	**abricot** (m)	[abriko]
raspberry	**framboise** (f)	[frɑ̃bwaz]
pineapple	**ananas** (m)	[anana]

banana	**banane** (f)	[banan]
watermelon	**pastèque** (f)	[pastɛk]
grape	**raisin** (m)	[rɛzɛ̃]
sour cherry	**cerise** (f)	[səriz]
sweet cherry	**merise** (f)	[məriz]
melon	**melon** (m)	[məlɔ̃]

grapefruit	**pamplemousse** (m)	[pɑ̃pləmus]
avocado	**avocat** (m)	[avɔka]

papaya	papaye (f)	[papaj]
mango	mangue (f)	[mɑ̃g]
pomegranate	grenade (f)	[grənad]

redcurrant	groseille (f) rouge	[grozɛj ruʒ]
blackcurrant	cassis (m)	[kasis]
gooseberry	groseille (f) verte	[grozɛj vɛrt]
bilberry	myrtille (f)	[mirtij]
blackberry	mûre (f)	[myr]

raisin	raisin (m) sec	[rɛzɛ̃ sɛk]
fig	figue (f)	[fig]
date	datte (f)	[dat]

peanut	cacahuète (f)	[kakawɛt]
almond	amande (f)	[amɑ̃d]
walnut	noix (f)	[nwa]
hazelnut	noisette (f)	[nwazɛt]
coconut	noix (f) de coco	[nwa də kɔkɔ]
pistachios	pistaches (f pl)	[pistaʃ]

56. Bread. Candy

bakers' confectionery (pastry)	confiserie (f)	[kɔ̃fizri]
bread	pain (m)	[pɛ̃]
cookies	biscuit (m)	[biskɥi]

chocolate (n)	chocolat (m)	[ʃɔkɔla]
chocolate (as adj)	en chocolat (adj)	[ɑ̃ ʃɔkɔla]
candy	bonbon (m)	[bɔ̃bɔ̃]
cake (e.g., cupcake)	gâteau (m)	[gato]
cake (e.g., birthday ~)	tarte (f)	[tart]

| pie (e.g., apple ~) | gâteau (m) | [gato] |
| filling (for cake, pie) | garniture (f) | [garnityr] |

whole fruit jam	confiture (f)	[kɔ̃fityr]
marmalade	marmelade (f)	[marmelad]
waffles	gaufre (f)	[gofr]
ice-cream	glace (f)	[glas]
pudding	pudding (m)	[pudiŋ]

57. Spices

salt	sel (m)	[sɛl]
salty (adj)	salé (adj)	[sale]
to salt (vt)	saler (vt)	[sale]

black pepper	**poivre** (m) **noir**	[pwavr nwar]
red pepper (milled ~)	**poivre** (m) **rouge**	[pwavr ruʒ]
mustard	**moutarde** (f)	[mutard]
horseradish	**raifort** (m)	[rɛfɔr]
condiment	**condiment** (m)	[kɔ̃dimɑ̃]
spice	**épice** (f)	[epis]
sauce	**sauce** (f)	[sos]
vinegar	**vinaigre** (m)	[vinɛgr]
anise	**anis** (m)	[ani(s)]
basil	**basilic** (m)	[bazilik]
cloves	**clou** (m) **de girofle**	[klu də ʒirɔfl]
ginger	**gingembre** (m)	[ʒɛ̃ʒɑ̃br]
coriander	**coriandre** (m)	[kɔrjɑ̃dr]
cinnamon	**cannelle** (f)	[kanɛl]
sesame	**sésame** (m)	[sezam]
bay leaf	**feuille** (f) **de laurier**	[fœj də lɔrje]
paprika	**paprika** (m)	[paprika]
caraway	**cumin** (m)	[kymɛ̃]
saffron	**safran** (m)	[safrɑ̃]

PERSONAL INFORMATION. FAMILY

T&P Books Publishing

58. Personal information. Forms

name (first name)	**prénom** (m)	[prenɔ̃]
surname (last name)	**nom** (m) **de famille**	[nɔ̃ də famij]
date of birth	**date** (f) **de naissance**	[dat də nɛsɑ̃s]
place of birth	**lieu** (m) **de naissance**	[ljø də nɛsɑ̃s]
nationality	**nationalité** (f)	[nasjɔnalite]
place of residence	**domicile** (m)	[dɔmisil]
country	**pays** (m)	[pei]
profession (occupation)	**profession** (f)	[prɔfɛsjɔ̃]
gender, sex	**sexe** (m)	[sɛks]
height	**taille** (f)	[taj]
weight	**poids** (m)	[pwa]

59. Family members. Relatives

mother	**mère** (f)	[mɛr]
father	**père** (m)	[pɛr]
son	**fils** (m)	[fis]
daughter	**fille** (f)	[fij]
younger daughter	**fille** (f) **cadette**	[fij kadɛt]
younger son	**fils** (m) **cadet**	[fis kadɛ]
eldest daughter	**fille** (f) **aînée**	[fij ene]
eldest son	**fils** (m) **aîné**	[fis ene]
brother	**frère** (m)	[frɛr]
sister	**sœur** (f)	[sœr]
cousin (masc.)	**cousin** (m)	[kuzɛ̃]
cousin (fem.)	**cousine** (f)	[kuzin]
mom, mommy	**maman** (f)	[mamɑ̃]
dad, daddy	**papa** (m)	[papa]
parents	**parents** (pl)	[parɑ̃]
child	**enfant** (m, f)	[ɑ̃fɑ̃]
children	**enfants** (pl)	[ɑ̃fɑ̃]
grandmother	**grand-mère** (f)	[grɑ̃mɛr]
grandfather	**grand-père** (m)	[grɑ̃pɛr]
grandson	**petit-fils** (m)	[pti fis]
granddaughter	**petite-fille** (f)	[ptit fij]
grandchildren	**petits-enfants** (pl)	[pətizɑ̃fɑ̃]

uncle	oncle (m)	[ɔ̃kl]
aunt	tante (f)	[tɑ̃t]
nephew	neveu (m)	[nəvø]
niece	nièce (f)	[njɛs]

mother-in-law (wife's mother)	belle-mère (f)	[bɛlmɛr]
father-in-law (husband's father)	beau-père (m)	[bopɛr]
son-in-law (daughter's husband)	gendre (m)	[ʒɑ̃dr]
stepmother	belle-mère, marâtre (f)	[bɛlmɛr], [marɑtr]
stepfather	beau-père (m)	[bopɛr]

infant	nourrisson (m)	[nurisɔ̃]
baby (infant)	bébé (m)	[bebe]
little boy, kid	petit (m)	[pti]

wife	femme (f)	[fam]
husband	mari (m)	[mari]
spouse (husband)	époux (m)	[epu]
spouse (wife)	épouse (f)	[epuz]

married (masc.)	marié (adj)	[marje]
married (fem.)	mariée (adj)	[marje]
single (unmarried)	célibataire (adj)	[selibatɛr]
bachelor	célibataire (m)	[selibatɛr]
divorced (masc.)	divorcé (adj)	[divɔrse]
widow	veuve (f)	[vœv]
widower	veuf (m)	[vœf]

relative	parent (m)	[parɑ̃]
close relative	parent (m) proche	[parɑ̃ prɔʃ]
distant relative	parent (m) éloigné	[parɑ̃ elwaɲe]
relatives	parents (m pl)	[parɑ̃]

orphan (boy)	orphelin (m)	[ɔrfəlɛ̃]
orphan (girl)	orpheline (f)	[ɔrfəlin]
guardian (of minor)	tuteur (m)	[tytœr]
to adopt (a boy)	adopter (vt)	[adɔpte]
to adopt (a girl)	adopter (vt)	[adɔpte]

60. Friends. Coworkers

friend (masc.)	ami (m)	[ami]
friend (fem.)	amie (f)	[ami]
friendship	amitié (f)	[amitje]
to be friends	être ami	[ɛtr ami]
buddy (masc.)	copain (m)	[kɔpɛ̃]
buddy (fem.)	copine (f)	[kɔpin]

partner	**partenaire** (m)	[partənɛr]
chief (boss)	**chef** (m)	[ʃɛf]
superior (n)	**supérieur** (m)	[syperjœr]
owner, proprietor	**propriétaire** (m)	[prɔprijetɛr]
subordinate (n)	**subordonné** (m)	[sybɔrdɔne]
colleague	**collègue** (m, f)	[kɔlɛg]

acquaintance (person)	**connaissance** (f)	[kɔnɛsɑ̃s]
fellow traveler	**compagnon** (m) **de route**	[kɔ̃paɲɔ̃ də rut]
classmate	**copain** (m) **de classe**	[kɔpɛ̃ də klas]

neighbor (masc.)	**voisin** (m)	[vwazɛ̃]
neighbor (fem.)	**voisine** (f)	[vwazin]
neighbors	**voisins** (m pl)	[vwazɛ̃]

T&P BOOKS

HUMAN BODY. MEDICINE

T&P Books Publishing

head	tête (f)	[tɛt]
face	visage (m)	[vizaʒ]
nose	nez (m)	[ne]
mouth	bouche (f)	[buʃ]

eye	œil (m)	[œj]
eyes	les yeux	[lezjø]
pupil	pupille (f)	[pypij]
eyebrow	sourcil (m)	[sursi]
eyelash	cil (m)	[sil]
eyelid	paupière (f)	[popjɛr]

tongue	langue (f)	[lɑ̃g]
tooth	dent (f)	[dɑ̃]
lips	lèvres (f pl)	[lɛvr]
cheekbones	pommettes (f pl)	[pɔmɛt]
gum	gencive (f)	[ʒɑ̃siv]
palate	palais (m)	[palɛ]

nostrils	narines (f pl)	[narin]
chin	menton (m)	[mɑ̃tɔ̃]
jaw	mâchoire (f)	[mɑʃwar]
cheek	joue (f)	[ʒu]

forehead	front (m)	[frɔ̃]
temple	tempe (f)	[tɑ̃p]
ear	oreille (f)	[ɔrɛj]
back of the head	nuque (f)	[nyk]
neck	cou (m)	[ku]
throat	gorge (f)	[gɔrʒ]

hair	cheveux (m pl)	[ʃəvø]
hairstyle	coiffure (f)	[kwafyr]
haircut	coupe (f)	[kup]
wig	perruque (f)	[peryk]

mustache	moustache (f)	[mustaʃ]
beard	barbe (f)	[barb]
to have (a beard, etc.)	porter (vt)	[pɔrte]
braid	tresse (f)	[trɛs]
sideburns	favoris (m pl)	[favɔri]

red-haired (adj)	roux (adj)	[ru]
gray (hair)	gris (adj)	[gri]

| bald (adj) | chauve (adj) | [ʃov] |
| bald patch | calvitie (f) | [kalvisi] |

| ponytail | queue (f) de cheval | [kø də ʃəval] |
| bangs | frange (f) | [frɑ̃ʒ] |

62. Human body

| hand | main (f) | [mɛ̃] |
| arm | bras (m) | [bra] |

finger	doigt (m)	[dwa]
toe	orteil (m)	[ɔrtɛj]
thumb	pouce (m)	[pus]
little finger	petit doigt (m)	[pəti dwa]
nail	ongle (m)	[ɔ̃gl]

fist	poing (m)	[pwɛ̃]
palm	paume (f)	[pom]
wrist	poignet (m)	[pwaɲɛ]
forearm	avant-bras (m)	[avɑ̃bra]
elbow	coude (m)	[kud]
shoulder	épaule (f)	[epol]

leg	jambe (f)	[ʒɑ̃b]
foot	pied (m)	[pje]
knee	genou (m)	[ʒənu]
calf (part of leg)	mollet (m)	[mɔlɛ]
hip	hanche (f)	[ɑ̃ʃ]
heel	talon (m)	[talɔ̃]

body	corps (m)	[kɔr]
stomach	ventre (m)	[vɑ̃tr]
chest	poitrine (f)	[pwatrin]
breast	sein (m)	[sɛ̃]
flank	côté (m)	[kote]
back	dos (m)	[do]
lower back	reins (m pl),	[rɛ̃], [reʒjɔ̃
	région (f) lombaire	lɔ̃bɛr]
waist	taille (f)	[taj]

navel (belly button)	nombril (m)	[nɔ̃bril]
buttocks	fesses (f pl)	[fɛs]
bottom	derrière (m)	[dɛrjɛr]

beauty mark	grain (m) de beauté	[grɛ̃ də bote]
birthmark	tache (f) de vin	[taʃ də vɛ̃]
(café au lait spot)		
tattoo	tatouage (m)	[tatwaʒ]
scar	cicatrice (f)	[sikatris]

63. Diseases

sickness	maladie (f)	[maladi]
to be sick	être malade	[εtr malad]
health	santé (f)	[sɑ̃te]

runny nose (coryza)	rhume (m)	[rym]
tonsillitis	angine (f)	[ɑ̃ʒin]
cold (illness)	refroidissement (m)	[rəfrwadismɑ̃]
to catch a cold	prendre froid	[prɑ̃dr frwa]

bronchitis	bronchite (f)	[brɔ̃ʃit]
pneumonia	pneumonie (f)	[pnømɔni]
flu, influenza	grippe (f)	[grip]

nearsighted (adj)	myope (adj)	[mjɔp]
farsighted (adj)	presbyte (adj)	[prεsbit]
strabismus (crossed eyes)	strabisme (m)	[strabism]
cross-eyed (adj)	strabique (adj)	[strabik]
cataract	cataracte (f)	[katarakt]
glaucoma	glaucome (m)	[glokom]

stroke	insulte (f)	[ε̃sylt]
heart attack	crise (f) cardiaque	[kriz kardjak]
myocardial infarction	infarctus (m) de myocarde	[ε̃farktys də mjɔkard]
paralysis	paralysie (f)	[paralizi]
to paralyze (vt)	paralyser (vt)	[paralize]

allergy	allergie (f)	[alεrʒi]
asthma	asthme (m)	[asm]
diabetes	diabète (m)	[djabεt]

toothache	mal (m) de dents	[mal də dɑ̃]
caries	carie (f)	[kari]

diarrhea	diarrhée (f)	[djare]
constipation	constipation (f)	[kɔ̃stipasjɔ̃]
stomach upset	estomac (m) barbouillé	[εstɔma barbuje]
food poisoning	intoxication (f) alimentaire	[ε̃tɔksikasjɔn alimɑ̃tεr]
to get food poisoning	être intoxiqué	[εtr ε̃tɔksike]

arthritis	arthrite (f)	[artrit]
rickets	rachitisme (m)	[raʃitism]
rheumatism	rhumatisme (m)	[rymatism]
atherosclerosis	athérosclérose (f)	[ateroskleroz]

gastritis	gastrite (f)	[gastrit]
appendicitis	appendicite (f)	[apε̃disit]
cholecystitis	cholécystite (f)	[kɔlesistit]

ulcer	ulcère (m)	[ylsɛr]
measles	rougeole (f)	[ruʒɔl]
rubella (German measles)	rubéole (f)	[rybeɔl]
jaundice	jaunisse (f)	[ʒonis]
hepatitis	hépatite (f)	[epatit]

schizophrenia	schizophrénie (f)	[skizɔfreni]
rabies (hydrophobia)	rage (f)	[raʒ]
neurosis	névrose (f)	[nevroz]
concussion	commotion (f) cérébrale	[kɔmɔsjɔ̃ serebral]

cancer	cancer (m)	[kɑ̃sɛr]
sclerosis	sclérose (f)	[skleroz]
multiple sclerosis	sclérose (f) en plaques	[skleroz ɑ̃ plak]

alcoholism	alcoolisme (m)	[alkɔlism]
alcoholic (n)	alcoolique (m)	[alkɔlik]
syphilis	syphilis (f)	[sifilis]
AIDS	SIDA (m)	[sida]

tumor	tumeur (f)	[tymœr]
malignant (adj)	maligne (adj)	[maliɲ]
benign (adj)	bénigne (adj)	[beniɲ]

fever	fièvre (f)	[fjɛvr]
malaria	malaria (f)	[malarja]
gangrene	gangrène (f)	[gɑ̃grɛn]
seasickness	mal (m) de mer	[mal də mɛr]
epilepsy	épilepsie (f)	[epilɛpsi]

epidemic	épidémie (f)	[epidemi]
typhus	typhus (m)	[tifys]
tuberculosis	tuberculose (f)	[tybɛrkyloz]
cholera	choléra (m)	[kɔlera]
plague (bubonic ~)	peste (f)	[pɛst]

64. Symptoms. Treatments. Part 1

symptom	symptôme (m)	[sɛ̃ptom]
temperature	température (f)	[tɑ̃peratyr]
high temperature (fever)	fièvre (f)	[fjɛvr]
pulse	pouls (m)	[pu]

dizziness (vertigo)	vertige (m)	[vɛrtiʒ]
hot (adj)	chaud (adj)	[ʃo]
shivering	frisson (m)	[frisɔ̃]
pale (e.g., ~ face)	pâle (adj)	[pɑl]
cough	toux (f)	[tu]
to cough (vi)	tousser (vi)	[tuse]

to sneeze (vi)	éternuer (vi)	[etɛrnɥe]
faint	évanouissement (m)	[evanwismɑ̃]
to faint (vi)	s'évanouir (vp)	[sevanwir]

bruise (hématome)	bleu (m)	[blø]
bump (lump)	bosse (f)	[bɔs]
to bang (bump)	se heurter (vp)	[sə œrte]
contusion (bruise)	meurtrissure (f)	[mœrtrisyr]
to get a bruise	se faire mal	[sə fɛr mal]

to limp (vi)	boiter (vi)	[bwate]
dislocation	foulure (f)	[fulyr]
to dislocate (vt)	se démettre (vp)	[sə demɛtr]
fracture	fracture (f)	[fraktyr]
to have a fracture	avoir une fracture	[avwar yn fraktyr]

cut (e.g., paper ~)	coupure (f)	[kupyr]
to cut oneself	se couper (vp)	[sə kupe]
bleeding	hémorragie (f)	[emɔraʒi]

burn (injury)	brûlure (f)	[brylyr]
to get burned	se brûler (vp)	[sə bryle]

to prick (vt)	se piquer (vp)	[sə pike]
to prick oneself	se piquer (vp)	[sə pike]
to injure (vt)	blesser (vt)	[blese]
injury	blessure (f)	[blesyr]
wound	blessure (f)	[blesyr]
trauma	trauma (m)	[troma]

to be delirious	délirer (vi)	[delire]
to stutter (vi)	bégayer (vi)	[begeje]
sunstroke	insolation (f)	[ɛ̃sɔlasjɔ̃]

65. Symptoms. Treatments. Part 2

pain	douleur (f)	[dulœr]
splinter (in foot, etc.)	écharde (f)	[eʃard]

sweat (perspiration)	sueur (f)	[sɥœr]
to sweat (perspire)	suer (vi)	[sɥe]
vomiting	vomissement (m)	[vɔmismɑ̃]
convulsions	spasmes (m pl)	[spasm]

pregnant (adj)	enceinte (adj)	[ɑ̃sɛ̃t]
to be born	naître (vi)	[nɛtr]
delivery, labor	accouchement (m)	[akuʃmɑ̃]
to deliver (~ a baby)	accoucher (vt)	[akuʃe]
abortion	avortement (m)	[avɔrtəmɑ̃]
breathing, respiration	respiration (f)	[rɛspirasjɔ̃]

in-breath (inhalation)	inhalation (f)	[inalasjɔ̃]
out-breath (exhalation)	expiration (f)	[ɛkspirasjɔ̃]
to exhale (breathe out)	expirer (vi)	[ɛkspire]
to inhale (vi)	inspirer (vi)	[inale]

disabled person	invalide (m)	[ɛ̃valid]
cripple	handicapé (m)	[ɑ̃dikape]
drug addict	drogué (m)	[drɔge]

deaf (adj)	sourd (adj)	[sur]
mute (adj)	muet (adj)	[mчɛ]
deaf mute (adj)	sourd-muet (adj)	[surmчɛ]

mad, insane (adj)	fou (adj)	[fu]
madman	fou (m)	[fu]
(demented person)		
madwoman	folle (f)	[fɔl]
to go insane	devenir fou	[dəvnir fu]

gene	gène (m)	[ʒɛn]
immunity	immunité (f)	[imynite]
hereditary (adj)	héréditaire (adj)	[ereditɛr]
congenital (adj)	congénital (adj)	[kɔ̃ʒenital]

virus	virus (m)	[virys]
microbe	microbe (m)	[mikrɔb]
bacterium	bactérie (f)	[bakteri]
infection	infection (f)	[ɛ̃fɛksjɔ̃]

66. Symptoms. Treatments. Part 3

| hospital | hôpital (m) | [ɔpital] |
| patient | patient (m) | [pasjɑ̃] |

diagnosis	diagnostic (m)	[djagnɔstik]
cure	cure (f)	[kyr]
medical treatment	traitement (m)	[trɛtmɑ̃]
to get treatment	se faire soigner	[sə fɛr swaɲe]
to treat (~ a patient)	traiter (vt)	[trete]
to nurse (look after)	soigner (vt)	[swaɲe]
care (nursing ~)	soins (m pl)	[swɛ̃]

operation, surgery	opération (f)	[ɔperasjɔ̃]
to bandage (head, limb)	panser (vt)	[pɑ̃se]
bandaging	pansement (m)	[pɑ̃smɑ̃]

vaccination	vaccination (f)	[vaksinasjɔ̃]
to vaccinate (vt)	vacciner (vt)	[vaksine]
injection, shot	piqûre (f)	[pikyr]
to give an injection	faire une piqûre	[fɛr yn pikyr]

attack	crise, attaque (f)	[kriz], [atak]
amputation	amputation (f)	[ɑ̃pytasjɔ̃]
to amputate (vt)	amputer (vt)	[ɑ̃pyte]
coma	coma (m)	[kɔma]
to be in a coma	être dans le coma	[ɛtr dɑ̃ lə kɔma]
intensive care	réanimation (f)	[reanimasjɔ̃]

to recover (~ from flu)	se rétablir (vp)	[sə retablir]
condition (patient's ~)	état (m)	[eta]
consciousness	conscience (f)	[kɔ̃sjɑ̃s]
memory (faculty)	mémoire (f)	[memwar]

to pull out (tooth)	arracher (vt)	[araʃe]
filling	plombage (m)	[plɔ̃baʒ]
to fill (a tooth)	plomber (vt)	[plɔ̃be]

| hypnosis | hypnose (f) | [ipnoz] |
| to hypnotize (vt) | hypnotiser (vt) | [ipnɔtize] |

67. Medicine. Drugs. Accessories

medicine, drug	médicament (m)	[medikamɑ̃]
remedy	remède (m)	[rəmɛd]
to prescribe (vt)	prescrire (vt)	[prɛskrir]
prescription	ordonnance (f)	[ɔrdɔnɑ̃s]

tablet, pill	comprimé (m)	[kɔ̃prime]
ointment	onguent (m)	[ɔ̃gɑ̃]
ampule	ampoule (f)	[ɑ̃pul]
mixture	mixture (f)	[mikstyr]
syrup	sirop (m)	[siro]
pill	pilule (f)	[pilyl]
powder	poudre (f)	[pudr]

gauze bandage	bande (f)	[bɑ̃d]
cotton wool	coton (m)	[kɔtɔ̃]
iodine	iode (m)	[jɔd]
Band-Aid	sparadrap (m)	[sparadra]
eyedropper	compte-gouttes (m)	[kɔ̃tgut]
thermometer	thermomètre (m)	[tɛrmɔmɛtr]
syringe	seringue (f)	[sərɛ̃g]

| wheelchair | fauteuil (m) roulant | [fotœj rulɑ̃] |
| crutches | béquilles (f pl) | [bekij] |

painkiller	anesthésique (m)	[anɛstezik]
laxative	purgatif (m)	[pyrgatif]
spirits (ethanol)	alcool (m)	[alkɔl]
medicinal herbs	herbe (f) médicinale	[ɛrb medisinal]
herbal (~ tea)	d'herbes (adj)	[dɛrb]

APARTMENT

68. Apartment

apartment	**appartement** (m)	[apartəmɑ̃]
room	**chambre** (f)	[ʃɑ̃br]
bedroom	**chambre** (f) **à coucher**	[ʃɑ̃br ɑ kuʃe]
dining room	**salle** (f) **à manger**	[sal ɑ mɑ̃ʒe]
living room	**salon** (m)	[salɔ̃]
study (home office)	**bureau** (m)	[byro]
entry room	**antichambre** (f)	[ɑ̃tiʃɑ̃br]
bathroom (room with a bath or shower)	**salle** (f) **de bains**	[sal də bɛ̃]
half bath	**toilettes** (f pl)	[twalɛt]
ceiling	**plafond** (m)	[plafɔ̃]
floor	**plancher** (m)	[plɑ̃ʃe]
corner	**coin** (m)	[kwɛ̃]

69. Furniture. Interior

furniture	**meubles** (m pl)	[mœbl]
table	**table** (f)	[tabl]
chair	**chaise** (f)	[ʃɛz]
bed	**lit** (m)	[li]
couch, sofa	**canapé** (m)	[kanape]
armchair	**fauteuil** (m)	[fotœj]
bookcase	**bibliothèque** (f)	[biblijɔtɛk]
shelf	**rayon** (m)	[rɛjɔ̃]
shelving unit	**étagère** (f)	[etaʒɛr]
wardrobe	**armoire** (f)	[armwar]
coat rack (wall-mounted ~)	**patère** (f)	[patɛr]
coat stand	**portemanteau** (m)	[pɔrtmɑ̃to]
bureau, dresser	**commode** (f)	[kɔmɔd]
coffee table	**table** (f) **basse**	[tabl bas]
mirror	**miroir** (m)	[mirwar]
carpet	**tapis** (m)	[tapi]
rug, small carpet	**petit tapis** (m)	[pəti tapi]
fireplace	**cheminée** (f)	[ʃəmine]
candle	**bougie** (f)	[buʒi]

candlestick	chandelier (m)	[ʃɑ̃dəlje]
drapes	rideaux (m pl)	[rido]
wallpaper	papier (m) peint	[papje pɛ̃]
blinds (jalousie)	jalousie (f)	[ʒaluzi]

table lamp	lampe (f) de table	[lɑ̃p də tabl]
wall lamp (sconce)	applique (f)	[aplik]
floor lamp	lampadaire (m)	[lɑ̃padɛr]
chandelier	lustre (m)	[lystr]

leg (of chair, table)	pied (m)	[pje]
armrest	accoudoir (m)	[akudwar]
back (backrest)	dossier (m)	[dosje]
drawer	tiroir (m)	[tirwar]

70. Bedding

bedclothes	linge (m) de lit	[lɛ̃ʒ də li]
pillow	oreiller (m)	[ɔrɛje]
pillowcase	taie (f) d'oreiller	[tɛ dɔrɛje]
duvet, comforter	couverture (f)	[kuvɛrtyr]
sheet	drap (m)	[dra]
bedspread	couvre-lit (m)	[kuvrəli]

71. Kitchen

kitchen	cuisine (f)	[kɥizin]
gas	gaz (m)	[gaz]
gas stove (range)	cuisinière (f) à gaz	[kɥizinjɛr a gaz]
electric stove	cuisinière (f) électrique	[kɥizinjɛr elɛktrik]
oven	four (m)	[fur]
microwave oven	four (m) micro-ondes	[fur mikrɔɔ̃d]

refrigerator	réfrigérateur (m)	[refriʒeratœr]
freezer	congélateur (m)	[kɔ̃ʒelatœr]
dishwasher	lave-vaisselle (m)	[lavvesɛl]

meat grinder	hachoir (m)	[aʃwar]
juicer	centrifugeuse (f)	[sɑ̃trifyʒøz]
toaster	grille-pain (m)	[grijpɛ̃]
mixer	batteur (m)	[batœr]

coffee machine	machine (f) à café	[maʃin a kafe]
coffee pot	cafetière (f)	[kaftjɛr]
coffee grinder	moulin (m) à café	[mulɛ̃ a kafe]

| kettle | bouilloire (f) | [bujwar] |
| teapot | théière (f) | [tejɛr] |

lid	couvercle (m)	[kuvɛrkl]
tea strainer	passoire (f) à thé	[paswar a te]
spoon	cuillère (f)	[kɥijɛr]
teaspoon	petite cuillère (f)	[pətit kɥijɛr]
soup spoon	cuillère (f) à soupe	[kɥijɛr a sup]
fork	fourchette (f)	[furʃɛt]
knife	couteau (m)	[kuto]
tableware (dishes)	vaisselle (f)	[vɛsɛl]
plate (dinner ~)	assiette (f)	[asjɛt]
saucer	soucoupe (f)	[sukup]
shot glass	verre (m) à shot	[vɛr a ʃot]
glass (tumbler)	verre (m)	[vɛr]
cup	tasse (f)	[tɑs]
sugar bowl	sucrier (m)	[sykrije]
salt shaker	salière (f)	[saljɛr]
pepper shaker	poivrière (f)	[pwavrijɛr]
butter dish	beurrier (m)	[bœrje]
stock pot (soup pot)	casserole (f)	[kasrɔl]
frying pan (skillet)	poêle (f)	[pwal]
ladle	louche (f)	[luʃ]
colander	passoire (f)	[paswar]
tray (serving ~)	plateau (m)	[plato]
bottle	bouteille (f)	[butɛj]
jar (glass)	bocal (m)	[bɔkal]
can	boîte (f) en fer-blanc	[bwat ɑ̃ fɛrblɑ̃]
bottle opener	ouvre-bouteille (m)	[uvrəbutɛj]
can opener	ouvre-boîte (m)	[uvrəbwat]
corkscrew	tire-bouchon (m)	[tirbuʃɔ̃]
filter	filtre (m)	[filtr]
to filter (vt)	filtrer (vt)	[filtre]
trash, garbage (food waste, etc.)	ordures (f pl)	[ɔrdyr]
trash can (kitchen ~)	poubelle (f)	[pubɛl]

72. Bathroom

bathroom	salle (f) de bains	[sal də bɛ̃]
water	eau (f)	[o]
faucet	robinet (m)	[rɔbinɛ]
hot water	eau (f) chaude	[o ʃod]
cold water	eau (f) froide	[o frwad]
toothpaste	dentifrice (m)	[dɑ̃tifris]

| to brush one's teeth | se brosser les dents | [sə brɔse le dɑ̃] |
| toothbrush | brosse (f) à dents | [brɔs ɑ dɑ̃] |

to shave (vi)	se raser (vp)	[sə raze]
shaving foam	mousse (f) à raser	[mus ɑ raze]
razor	rasoir (m)	[razwar]

to wash (one's hands, etc.)	laver (vt)	[lave]
to take a bath	se laver (vp)	[sə lave]
shower	douche (f)	[duʃ]
to take a shower	prendre une douche	[prɑ̃dr yn duʃ]

bathtub	baignoire (f)	[bɛɲwar]
toilet (toilet bowl)	cuvette (f)	[kyvɛt]
sink (washbasin)	lavabo (m)	[lavabo]

| soap | savon (m) | [savɔ̃] |
| soap dish | porte-savon (m) | [pɔrtsavɔ̃] |

sponge	éponge (f)	[epɔ̃ʒ]
shampoo	shampooing (m)	[ʃɑ̃pwɛ̃]
towel	serviette (f)	[sɛrvjɛt]
bathrobe	peignoir (m) de bain	[pɛɲwar də bɛ̃]

laundry (process)	lessive (f)	[lɛsiv]
washing machine	machine (f) à laver	[maʃin ɑ lave]
to do the laundry	faire la lessive	[fɛr la lɛsiv]
laundry detergent	lessive (f)	[lɛsiv]

73. Household appliances

TV set	télé (f)	[tele]
tape recorder	magnétophone (m)	[maɲetɔfɔn]
VCR (video recorder)	magnétoscope (m)	[maɲetɔskɔp]
radio	radio (f)	[radjo]
player (CD, MP3, etc.)	lecteur (m)	[lɛktœr]

video projector	vidéoprojecteur (m)	[videɔprɔʒɛktœr]
home movie theater	home cinéma (m)	[həʊm sinema]
DVD player	lecteur DVD (m)	[lɛktœr devede]
amplifier	amplificateur (m)	[ɑ̃plifikatœr]
video game console	console (f) de jeux	[kɔ̃sɔl də ʒø]

video camera	caméscope (m)	[kameskɔp]
camera (photo)	appareil (m) photo	[aparɛj fɔto]
digital camera	appareil (m) photo numérique	[aparɛj fɔto nymerik]

| vacuum cleaner | aspirateur (m) | [aspiratœr] |
| iron (e.g., steam ~) | fer (m) à repasser | [fɛr ɑ rəpase] |

ironing board	**planche** (f) **à repasser**	[plɑ̃ʃ ɑ rəpase]
telephone	**téléphone** (m)	[telefɔn]
mobile phone	**portable** (m)	[pɔrtabl]
typewriter	**machine** (f) **à écrire**	[maʃin ɑ ekrir]
sewing machine	**machine** (f) **à coudre**	[maʃin ɑ kudr]
microphone	**micro** (m)	[mikro]
headphones	**écouteurs** (m pl)	[ekutœr]
remote control (TV)	**télécommande** (f)	[telekɔmɑ̃d]
CD, compact disc	**CD** (m)	[sede]
cassette	**cassette** (f)	[kasɛt]
vinyl record	**disque** (m) **vinyle**	[disk vinil]

THE EARTH. WEATHER

T&P Books Publishing

74. Outer space

space	cosmos (m)	[kɔsmos]
space (as adj)	cosmique (adj)	[kɔsmik]
outer space	espace (m) cosmique	[ɛspas kɔsmik]
world	monde (m)	[mɔ̃d]
universe	univers (m)	[ynivɛr]
galaxy	galaxie (f)	[galaksi]
star	étoile (f)	[etwal]
constellation	constellation (f)	[kɔ̃stelasjɔ̃]
planet	planète (f)	[planɛt]
satellite	satellite (m)	[satelit]
meteorite	météorite (m)	[meteɔrit]
comet	comète (f)	[kɔmɛt]
asteroid	astéroïde (m)	[asterɔid]
orbit	orbite (f)	[ɔrbit]
to revolve	tourner (vi)	[turne]
(~ around the Earth)		
atmosphere	atmosphère (f)	[atmɔsfɛr]
the Sun	Soleil (m)	[sɔlɛj]
solar system	système (m) solaire	[sistɛm sɔlɛr]
solar eclipse	éclipse (f) de soleil	[leklips də sɔlɛj]
the Earth	Terre (f)	[tɛr]
the Moon	Lune (f)	[lyn]
Mars	Mars (m)	[mars]
Venus	Vénus (f)	[venys]
Jupiter	Jupiter (m)	[ʒypitɛr]
Saturn	Saturne (m)	[satyrn]
Mercury	Mercure (m)	[mɛrkyr]
Uranus	Uranus (m)	[yranys]
Neptune	Neptune	[nɛptyn]
Pluto	Pluton (m)	[plytɔ̃]
Milky Way	la Voie Lactée	[la vwa lakte]
Great Bear (Ursa Major)	la Grande Ours	[la grɑ̃d urs]
North Star	la Polaire	[la pɔlɛr]
Martian	martien (m)	[marsjɛ̃]
extraterrestrial (n)	extraterrestre (m)	[ɛkstratɛrɛstr]

| alien | alien (m) | [aljen] |
| flying saucer | soucoupe (f) volante | [sukup vɔlɑ̃t] |

spaceship	vaisseau (m) spatial	[vɛso spasjal]
space station	station (f) orbitale	[stasjɔ̃ ɔrbital]
blast-off	lancement (m)	[lɑ̃smɑ̃]

engine	moteur (m)	[mɔtœr]
nozzle	tuyère (f)	[tyjɛr]
fuel	carburant (m)	[karbyrɑ̃]

cockpit, flight deck	cabine (f)	[kabin]
antenna	antenne (f)	[ɑ̃tɛn]
porthole	hublot (m)	[yblo]
solar panel	batterie (f) solaire	[batri sɔlɛr]
spacesuit	scaphandre (m)	[skafɑ̃dr]

| weightlessness | apesanteur (f) | [apəzɑ̃tœr] |
| oxygen | oxygène (m) | [ɔksiʒɛn] |

| docking (in space) | arrimage (m) | [arimaʒ] |
| to dock (vi, vt) | s'arrimer à ... | [sarime a] |

observatory	observatoire (m)	[ɔpsɛrvatwar]
telescope	télescope (m)	[teleskɔp]
to observe (vt)	observer (vt)	[ɔpsɛrve]
to explore (vt)	explorer (vt)	[ɛksplɔre]

75. The Earth

the Earth	Terre (f)	[tɛr]
the globe (the Earth)	globe (m) terrestre	[glɔb tɛrɛstr]
planet	planète (f)	[planɛt]

atmosphere	atmosphère (f)	[atmɔsfɛr]
geography	géographie (f)	[ʒeɔgrafi]
nature	nature (f)	[natyr]

globe (table ~)	globe (m) de table	[glɔb də tabl]
map	carte (f)	[kart]
atlas	atlas (m)	[atlas]

Europe	Europe (f)	[ørɔp]
Asia	Asie (f)	[azi]
Africa	Afrique (f)	[afrik]
Australia	Australie (f)	[ostrali]

America	Amérique (f)	[amerik]
North America	Amérique (f) du Nord	[amerik dy nɔr]
South America	Amérique (f) du Sud	[amerik dy syd]

| Antarctica | l'Antarctique (m) | [lɑ̃tarktik] |
| the Arctic | l'Arctique (m) | [larktik] |

76. Cardinal directions

north	nord (m)	[nɔr]
to the north	vers le nord	[vɛr lə nɔr]
in the north	au nord	[onɔr]
northern (adj)	du nord (adj)	[dy nɔr]

south	sud (m)	[syd]
to the south	vers le sud	[vɛr lə syd]
in the south	au sud	[osyd]
southern (adj)	du sud (adj)	[dy syd]

west	ouest (m)	[wɛst]
to the west	vers l'occident	[vɛr lɔksidɑ̃]
in the west	à l'occident	[alɔksidɑ̃]
western (adj)	occidental (adj)	[ɔksidɑ̃tal]

east	est (m)	[ɛst]
to the east	vers l'orient	[vɛr lɔrjɑ̃]
in the east	à l'orient	[alɔrjɑ̃]
eastern (adj)	oriental (adj)	[ɔrjɑ̃tal]

77. Sea. Ocean

sea	mer (f)	[mɛr]
ocean	océan (m)	[ɔseɑ̃]
gulf (bay)	golfe (m)	[gɔlf]
straits	détroit (m)	[detrwa]

land (solid ground)	terre (f) ferme	[tɛr fɛrm]
continent (mainland)	continent (m)	[kɔ̃tinɑ̃]
island	île (f)	[il]
peninsula	presqu'île (f)	[prɛskil]
archipelago	archipel (m)	[arʃipɛl]

bay, cove	baie (f)	[bɛ]
harbor	port (m)	[pɔr]
lagoon	lagune (f)	[lagyn]
cape	cap (m)	[kap]

atoll	atoll (m)	[atɔl]
reef	récif (m)	[resif]
coral	corail (m)	[kɔraj]
coral reef	récif (m) de corail	[resif də kɔraj]
deep (adj)	profond (adj)	[prɔfɔ̃]

depth (deep water)	**profondeur** (f)	[prɔfɔ̃dœr]
abyss	**abîme** (m)	[abim]
trench (e.g., Mariana ~)	**fosse** (f) **océanique**	[fos ɔseanik]
current (Ocean ~)	**courant** (m)	[kurɑ̃]
to surround (bathe)	**baigner** (vt)	[beɲe]
shore	**littoral** (m)	[litɔral]
coast	**côte** (f)	[kot]
flow (flood tide)	**marée** (f) **haute**	[mare ot]
ebb (ebb tide)	**marée** (f) **basse**	[mare bas]
shoal	**banc** (m) **de sable**	[bɑ̃ də sabl]
bottom (~ of the sea)	**fond** (m)	[fɔ̃]
wave	**vague** (f)	[vag]
crest (~ of a wave)	**crête** (f) **de la vague**	[krɛt də la vag]
spume (sea foam)	**mousse** (f)	[mus]
storm (sea storm)	**tempête** (f) **en mer**	[tɑ̃pɛt ɑ̃mɛr]
hurricane	**ouragan** (m)	[uragɑ̃]
tsunami	**tsunami** (m)	[tsynami]
calm (dead ~)	**calme** (m)	[kalm]
quiet, calm (adj)	**calme** (adj)	[kalm]
pole	**pôle** (m)	[pol]
polar (adj)	**polaire** (adj)	[pɔlɛr]
latitude	**latitude** (f)	[latityd]
longitude	**longitude** (f)	[lɔ̃ʒityd]
parallel	**parallèle** (f)	[paralɛl]
equator	**équateur** (m)	[ekwatœr]
sky	**ciel** (m)	[sjɛl]
horizon	**horizon** (m)	[ɔrizɔ̃]
air	**air** (m)	[ɛr]
lighthouse	**phare** (m)	[far]
to dive (vi)	**plonger** (vi)	[plɔ̃ʒe]
to sink (ab. boat)	**sombrer** (vi)	[sɔ̃bre]
treasures	**trésor** (m)	[trezɔr]

78. Seas' and Oceans' names

Atlantic Ocean	**océan** (m) **Atlantique**	[ɔseɑn atlɑ̃tik]
Indian Ocean	**océan** (m) **Indien**	[ɔseɑn ɛ̃djɛ̃]
Pacific Ocean	**océan** (m) **Pacifique**	[ɔseɑ̃ pasifik]
Arctic Ocean	**océan** (m) **Glacial**	[ɔseɑ̃ glasjal]
Black Sea	**mer** (f) **Noire**	[mɛr nwar]
Red Sea	**mer** (f) **Rouge**	[mɛr ruʒ]

| Yellow Sea | mer (f) Jaune | [mɛr ʒon] |
| White Sea | mer (f) Blanche | [mɛr blɑ̃ʃ] |

Caspian Sea	mer (f) Caspienne	[mɛr kaspjɛn]
Dead Sea	mer (f) Morte	[mɛr mɔrt]
Mediterranean Sea	mer (f) Méditerranée	[mɛr meditɛrane]

| Aegean Sea | mer (f) Égée | [mɛr eʒe] |
| Adriatic Sea | mer (f) Adriatique | [mɛr adrijatik] |

Arabian Sea	mer (f) Arabique	[mɛr arabik]
Sea of Japan	mer (f) du Japon	[mɛr dy ʒapɔ̃]
Bering Sea	mer (f) de Béring	[mɛr də beriŋ]
South China Sea	mer (f) de Chine Méridionale	[mɛr də ʃin meridjɔnal]

Coral Sea	mer (f) de Corail	[mɛr də kɔraj]
Tasman Sea	mer (f) de Tasman	[mɛr də tasman]
Caribbean Sea	mer (f) Caraïbe	[mɛr karaib]

| Barents Sea | mer (f) de Barents | [mɛr də barɛ̃s] |
| Kara Sea | mer (f) de Kara | [mɛr də kara] |

North Sea	mer (f) du Nord	[mɛr dy nɔr]
Baltic Sea	mer (f) Baltique	[mɛr baltik]
Norwegian Sea	mer (f) de Norvège	[mɛr də nɔrvɛʒ]

79. Mountains

mountain	montagne (f)	[mɔ̃taɲ]
mountain range	chaîne (f) de montagnes	[ʃɛn də mɔ̃taɲ]
mountain ridge	crête (f)	[krɛt]

summit, top	sommet (m)	[sɔmɛ]
peak	pic (m)	[pik]
foot (~ of the mountain)	pied (m)	[pje]
slope (mountainside)	pente (f)	[pɑ̃t]

volcano	volcan (m)	[vɔlkɑ̃]
active volcano	volcan (m) actif	[vɔlkɑn aktif]
dormant volcano	volcan (m) éteint	[vɔlkɑn etɛ̃]

eruption	éruption (f)	[erypsjɔ̃]
crater	cratère (m)	[kratɛr]
magma	magma (m)	[magma]
lava	lave (f)	[lav]
molten (~ lava)	en fusion	[ɑ̃ fyzjɔ̃]

| canyon | canyon (m) | [kanjɔ̃] |
| gorge | défilé (m) | [defile] |

| crevice | crevasse (f) | [krəvas] |
| abyss (chasm) | précipice (m) | [presipis] |

pass, col	col (m)	[kɔl]
plateau	plateau (m)	[plato]
cliff	rocher (m)	[rɔʃe]
hill	colline (f)	[kɔlin]

glacier	glacier (m)	[glasje]
waterfall	chute (f) d'eau	[ʃyt do]
geyser	geyser (m)	[ʒɛzɛr]
lake	lac (m)	[lak]

plain	plaine (f)	[plɛn]
landscape	paysage (m)	[peizaʒ]
echo	écho (m)	[eko]

alpinist	alpiniste (m)	[alpinist]
rock climber	varappeur (m)	[varapœr]
to conquer (in climbing)	conquérir (vt)	[kɔ̃kerir]
climb (an easy ~)	ascension (f)	[asɑ̃sjɔ̃]

80. Mountains names

The Alps	Alpes (f pl)	[alp]
Mont Blanc	Mont Blanc (m)	[mɔ̃blɑ̃]
The Pyrenees	Pyrénées (f pl)	[pirene]

The Carpathians	Carpates (f pl)	[karpat]
The Ural Mountains	Monts Oural (m pl)	[mɔ̃ ural]
The Caucasus Mountains	Caucase (m)	[kokaz]
Mount Elbrus	Elbrous (m)	[ɛlbrys]

The Altai Mountains	Altaï (m)	[altaj]
The Tian Shan	Tian Chan (m)	[tjɑ̃ ʃɑ̃]
The Pamir Mountains	Pamir (m)	[pamir]
The Himalayas	Himalaya (m)	[imalaja]
Mount Everest	Everest (m)	[evrɛst]

| The Andes | Andes (f pl) | [ɑ̃d] |
| Mount Kilimanjaro | Kilimandjaro (m) | [kilimɑ̃dʒaro] |

81. Rivers

river	rivière (f), fleuve (m)	[rivjɛr], [flœv]
spring (natural source)	source (f)	[surs]
riverbed (river channel)	lit (m)	[li]
basin	bassin (m)	[basɛ̃]

to flow into ...	se jeter dans ...	[sə ʒəte dɑ̃]
tributary	affluent (m)	[aflyɑ̃]
bank (of river)	rive (f)	[riv]

current (stream)	courant (m)	[kurɑ̃]
downstream (adv)	en aval	[ɑn aval]
upstream (adv)	en amont	[ɑn amɔ̃]

inundation	inondation (f)	[inɔ̃dasjɔ̃]
flooding	les grandes crues	[le grɑ̃d kry]
to overflow (vi)	déborder (vt)	[debɔrde]
to flood (vt)	inonder (vt)	[inɔ̃de]

shallow (shoal)	bas-fond (m)	[bafɔ̃]
rapids	rapide (m)	[rapid]

dam	barrage (m)	[baraʒ]
canal	canal (m)	[kanal]
reservoir (artificial lake)	lac (m) de barrage	[lak də baraʒ]
sluice, lock	écluse (f)	[eklyz]

water body (pond, etc.)	plan (m) d'eau	[plɑ̃ do]
swamp (marshland)	marais (m)	[marɛ]
bog, marsh	fondrière (f)	[fɔ̃drijɛr]
whirlpool	tourbillon (m)	[turbijɔ̃]

stream (brook)	ruisseau (m)	[rᶣiso]
drinking (ab. water)	potable (adj)	[pɔtabl]
fresh (~ water)	douce (adj)	[dus]

ice	glace (f)	[glas]
to freeze over (ab. river, etc.)	être gelé	[ɛtr ʒəle]

82. Rivers' names

Seine	Seine (f)	[sɛn]
Loire	Loire (f)	[lwar]

Thames	Tamise (f)	[tamiz]
Rhine	Rhin (m)	[rɛ̃]
Danube	Danube (m)	[danyb]

Volga	Volga (f)	[vɔlga]
Don	Don (m)	[dɔ̃]
Lena	Lena (f)	[lena]

Yellow River	Huang He (m)	[waŋ e]
Yangtze	Yangzi Jiang (m)	[jɑ̃gzijɑ̃g]
Mekong	Mékong (m)	[mekɔ̃g]

Ganges	Gange (m)	[gɑ̃ʒ]
Nile River	Nil (m)	[nil]
Congo River	Congo (m)	[kɔ̃go]
Okavango River	Okavango (m)	[ɔkavangɔ]
Zambezi River	Zambèze (m)	[zɑ̃bɛz]
Limpopo River	Limpopo (m)	[limpɔpo]
Mississippi River	Mississippi (m)	[misisipi]

83. Forest

| forest, wood | forêt (f) | [fɔrɛ] |
| forest (as adj) | forestier (adj) | [fɔrɛstje] |

thick forest	fourré (m)	[fure]
grove	bosquet (m)	[bɔskɛ]
forest clearing	clairière (f)	[klɛrjɛr]

| thicket | broussailles (f pl) | [brusaj] |
| scrubland | taillis (m) | [taji] |

| footpath (troddenpath) | sentier (m) | [sɑ̃tje] |
| gully | ravin (m) | [ravɛ̃] |

tree	arbre (m)	[arbr]
leaf	feuille (f)	[fœj]
leaves (foliage)	feuillage (m)	[fœjaʒ]

fall of leaves	chute (f) de feuilles	[ʃyt də fœj]
to fall (ab. leaves)	tomber (vi)	[tɔ̃be]
top (of the tree)	sommet (m)	[sɔmɛ]

branch	rameau (m)	[ramo]
bough	branche (f)	[brɑ̃ʃ]
bud (on shrub, tree)	bourgeon (m)	[burʒɔ̃]
needle (of pine tree)	aiguille (f)	[egɥij]
pine cone	pomme (f) de pin	[pɔm də pɛ̃]

hollow (in a tree)	creux (m)	[krø]
nest	nid (m)	[ni]
burrow (animal hole)	terrier (m)	[tɛrje]

trunk	tronc (m)	[trɔ̃]
root	racine (f)	[rasin]
bark	écorce (f)	[ekɔrs]
moss	mousse (f)	[mus]

to uproot (remove trees or tree stumps)	déraciner (vt)	[derasine]
to chop down	abattre (vt)	[abatr]
to deforest (vt)	déboiser (vt)	[debwaze]

tree stump	**souche** (f)	[suʃ]
campfire	**feu** (m) **de bois**	[fø də bwa]
forest fire	**incendie** (m)	[ɛ̃sãdi]
to extinguish (vt)	**éteindre** (vt)	[etɛ̃dr]

forest ranger	**garde** (m) **forestier**	[gard fɔrɛstje]
protection	**protection** (f)	[prɔtɛksjɔ̃]
to protect (~ nature)	**protéger** (vt)	[prɔteʒe]
poacher	**braconnier** (m)	[brakɔnje]
steel trap	**piège** (m) **à mâchoires**	[pjɛʒ ɑ mɑʃwar]

to gather, to pick (vt)	**cueillir** (vt)	[kœjir]
to lose one's way	**s'égarer** (vp)	[segare]

84. Natural resources

natural resources	**ressources** (f pl) **naturelles**	[rəsurs natyrɛl]
minerals	**minéraux** (m pl)	[minero]
deposits	**gisement** (m)	[ʒizmã]
field (e.g., oilfield)	**champ** (m)	[ʃã]

to mine (extract)	**extraire** (vt)	[ɛkstrɛr]
mining (extraction)	**extraction** (f)	[ɛkstraksjɔ̃]
ore	**minerai** (m)	[minrɛ]
mine (e.g., for coal)	**mine** (f)	[min]
shaft (mine ~)	**puits** (m) **de mine**	[pɥi də min]
miner	**mineur** (m)	[minœr]

gas (natural ~)	**gaz** (m)	[gaz]
gas pipeline	**gazoduc** (m)	[gazɔdyk]

oil (petroleum)	**pétrole** (m)	[petrɔl]
oil pipeline	**pipeline** (m)	[piplin]
oil well	**tour** (f) **de forage**	[tur də foraʒ]
derrick (tower)	**derrick** (m)	[derik]
tanker	**pétrolier** (m)	[petrɔlje]

sand	**sable** (m)	[sabl]
limestone	**calcaire** (m)	[kalkɛr]
gravel	**gravier** (m)	[gravje]
peat	**tourbe** (f)	[turb]
clay	**argile** (f)	[arʒil]
coal	**charbon** (m)	[ʃarbɔ̃]

iron (ore)	**fer** (m)	[fɛr]
gold	**or** (m)	[ɔr]
silver	**argent** (m)	[arʒã]
nickel	**nickel** (m)	[nikɛl]
copper	**cuivre** (m)	[kɥivr]

zinc	zinc (m)	[zɛ̃g]
manganese	manganèse (m)	[mãganɛz]
mercury	mercure (m)	[mɛrkyr]
lead	plomb (m)	[plɔ̃]

mineral	minéral (m)	[mineral]
crystal	cristal (m)	[kristal]
marble	marbre (m)	[marbr]
uranium	uranium (m)	[yranjɔm]

85. Weather

weather	temps (m)	[tã]
weather forecast	météo (f)	[meteo]
temperature	température (f)	[tãperatyr]
thermometer	thermomètre (m)	[tɛrmɔmɛtr]
barometer	baromètre (m)	[barɔmɛtr]

humid (adj)	humide (adj)	[ymid]
humidity	humidité (f)	[ymidite]
heat (extreme ~)	chaleur (f)	[ʃalœr]
hot (torrid)	torride (adj)	[tɔrid]
it's hot	il fait très chaud	[il fɛ trɛ ʃo]

| it's warm | il fait chaud | [il fɛʃo] |
| warm (moderately hot) | chaud (adj) | [ʃo] |

| it's cold | il fait froid | [il fɛ frwa] |
| cold (adj) | froid (adj) | [frwa] |

sun	soleil (m)	[sɔlɛj]
to shine (vi)	briller (vi)	[brije]
sunny (day)	ensoleillé (adj)	[ãsɔleje]
to come up (vi)	se lever (vp)	[sə ləve]
to set (vi)	se coucher (vp)	[sə kuʃe]

cloud	nuage (m)	[nɥaʒ]
cloudy (adj)	nuageux (adj)	[nɥaʒø]
rain cloud	nuée (f)	[nɥe]
somber (gloomy)	sombre (adj)	[sɔ̃br]

rain	pluie (f)	[plɥi]
it's raining	il pleut	[il plø]
rainy (~ day, weather)	pluvieux (adj)	[plyvjø]
to drizzle (vi)	bruiner (v imp)	[brɥine]

pouring rain	pluie (f) torrentielle	[plɥi tɔrãsjɛl]
downpour	averse (f)	[avɛrs]
heavy (e.g., ~ rain)	forte (adj)	[fɔrt]
puddle	flaque (f)	[flak]

to get wet (in rain)	se faire mouiller	[sə fɛr muje]
fog (mist)	brouillard (m)	[brujar]
foggy	brumeux (adj)	[brymø]
snow	neige (f)	[nɛʒ]
it's snowing	il neige	[il nɛʒ]

86. Severe weather. Natural disasters

thunderstorm	orage (m)	[ɔraʒ]
lightning (~ strike)	éclair (m)	[eklɛr]
to flash (vi)	éclater (vi)	[eklate]
thunder	tonnerre (m)	[tɔnɛr]
to thunder (vi)	gronder (vi)	[grɔ̃de]
it's thundering	le tonnerre gronde	[lə tɔnɛr grɔ̃d]
hail	grêle (f)	[grɛl]
it's hailing	il grêle	[il grɛl]
to flood (vt)	inonder (vt)	[inɔ̃de]
flood, inundation	inondation (f)	[inɔ̃dasjɔ̃]
earthquake	tremblement (m) de terre	[trɑ̃bləmɑ̃ də tɛr]
tremor, quake	secousse (f)	[səkus]
epicenter	épicentre (m)	[episɑ̃tr]
eruption	éruption (f)	[erypsjɔ̃]
lava	lave (f)	[lav]
twister	tourbillon (m)	[turbijɔ̃]
tornado	tornade (f)	[tɔrnad]
typhoon	typhon (m)	[tifɔ̃]
hurricane	ouragan (m)	[uragɑ̃]
storm	tempête (f)	[tɑ̃pɛt]
tsunami	tsunami (m)	[tsynami]
cyclone	cyclone (m)	[siklon]
bad weather	intempéries (f pl)	[ɛ̃tɑ̃peri]
fire (accident)	incendie (m)	[ɛ̃sɑ̃di]
disaster	catastrophe (f)	[katastrɔf]
meteorite	météorite (m)	[meteɔrit]
avalanche	avalanche (f)	[avalɑ̃ʃ]
snowslide	éboulement (m)	[ebulmɑ̃]
blizzard	blizzard (m)	[blizar]
snowstorm	tempête (f) de neige	[tɑ̃pɛt də nɛʒ]

FAUNA

T&P Books Publishing

87. Mammals. Predators

predator	prédateur (m)	[predatœr]
tiger	tigre (m)	[tigr]
lion	lion (m)	[ljɔ̃]
wolf	loup (m)	[lu]
fox	renard (m)	[rənar]

jaguar	jaguar (m)	[ʒagwar]
leopard	léopard (m)	[leɔpar]
cheetah	guépard (m)	[gepar]

black panther	panthère (f)	[pɑ̃tɛr]
puma	puma (m)	[pyma]
snow leopard	léopard (m) de neiges	[leɔpar də nɛʒ]
lynx	lynx (m)	[lɛ̃ks]

coyote	coyote (m)	[kɔjɔt]
jackal	chacal (m)	[ʃakal]
hyena	hyène (f)	[jɛn]

88. Wild animals

| animal | animal (m) | [animal] |
| beast (animal) | bête (f) | [bɛt] |

squirrel	écureuil (m)	[ekyrœj]
hedgehog	hérisson (m)	[erisɔ̃]
hare	lièvre (m)	[ljɛvr]
rabbit	lapin (m)	[lapɛ̃]

badger	blaireau (m)	[blɛro]
raccoon	raton (m)	[ratɔ̃]
hamster	hamster (m)	[amstɛr]
marmot	marmotte (f)	[marmɔt]

mole	taupe (f)	[top]
mouse	souris (f)	[suri]
rat	rat (m)	[ra]
bat	chauve-souris (f)	[ʃovsuri]

ermine	hermine (f)	[ɛrmin]
sable	zibeline (f)	[ziblin]
marten	martre (f)	[martr]

| weasel | belette (f) | [bəlɛt] |
| mink | vison (m) | [vizɔ̃] |

| beaver | castor (m) | [kastɔr] |
| otter | loutre (f) | [lutr] |

horse	cheval (m)	[ʃəval]
moose	élan (m)	[elɑ̃]
deer	cerf (m)	[sɛr]
camel	chameau (m)	[ʃamo]

bison	bison (m)	[bizɔ̃]
aurochs	aurochs (m)	[orɔk]
buffalo	buffle (m)	[byfl]

zebra	zèbre (m)	[zɛbr]
antelope	antilope (f)	[ɑ̃tilɔp]
roe deer	chevreuil (m)	[ʃəvrœj]
fallow deer	biche (f)	[biʃ]
chamois	chamois (m)	[ʃamwa]
wild boar	sanglier (m)	[sɑ̃glije]

whale	baleine (f)	[balɛn]
seal	phoque (m)	[fɔk]
walrus	morse (m)	[mɔrs]
fur seal	ours (m) de mer	[urs də mɛr]
dolphin	dauphin (m)	[dofɛ̃]

bear	ours (m)	[urs]
polar bear	ours (m) blanc	[urs blɑ̃]
panda	panda (m)	[pɑ̃da]

monkey	singe (m)	[sɛ̃ʒ]
chimpanzee	chimpanzé (m)	[ʃɛ̃pɑ̃ze]
orangutan	orang-outang (m)	[ɔrɑ̃utɑ̃]
gorilla	gorille (m)	[gɔrij]
macaque	macaque (m)	[makak]
gibbon	gibbon (m)	[ʒibɔ̃]

| elephant | éléphant (m) | [elefɑ̃] |
| rhinoceros | rhinocéros (m) | [rinɔserɔs] |

| giraffe | girafe (f) | [ʒiraf] |
| hippopotamus | hippopotame (m) | [ipɔpɔtam] |

| kangaroo | kangourou (m) | [kɑ̃guru] |
| koala (bear) | koala (m) | [kɔala] |

mongoose	mangouste (f)	[mɑ̃gust]
chinchilla	chinchilla (m)	[ʃɛ̃ʃila]
skunk	mouffette (f)	[mufɛt]
porcupine	porc-épic (m)	[pɔrkepik]

89. Domestic animals

cat	**chat** (m)	[ʃa]
tomcat	**chat** (m)	[ʃa]
dog	**chien** (m)	[ʃjɛ̃]
horse	**cheval** (m)	[ʃəval]
stallion	**étalon** (m)	[etalɔ̃]
mare	**jument** (f)	[ʒymɑ̃]
cow	**vache** (f)	[vaʃ]
bull	**taureau** (m)	[tɔro]
ox	**bœuf** (m)	[bœf]
sheep (ewe)	**brebis** (f)	[brəbi]
ram	**mouton** (m)	[mutɔ̃]
goat	**chèvre** (f)	[ʃɛvr]
billy goat, he-goat	**bouc** (m)	[buk]
donkey	**âne** (m)	[ɑn]
mule	**mulet** (m)	[mylɛ]
pig, hog	**cochon** (m)	[kɔʃɔ̃]
piglet	**pourceau** (m)	[purso]
rabbit	**lapin** (m)	[lapɛ̃]
hen (chicken)	**poule** (f)	[pul]
rooster	**coq** (m)	[kɔk]
duck	**canard** (m)	[kanar]
drake	**canard** (m) **mâle**	[kanar mal]
goose	**oie** (f)	[wa]
tom turkey, gobbler	**dindon** (m)	[dɛ̃dɔ̃]
turkey (hen)	**dinde** (f)	[dɛ̃d]
domestic animals	**animaux** (m pl) **domestiques**	[animo dɔmɛstik]
tame (e.g., ~ hamster)	**apprivoisé** (adj)	[aprivwaze]
to tame (vt)	**apprivoiser** (vt)	[aprivwaze]
to breed (vt)	**élever** (vt)	[elve]
farm	**ferme** (f)	[fɛrm]
poultry	**volaille** (f)	[vɔlaj]
cattle	**bétail** (m)	[betaj]
herd (cattle)	**troupeau** (m)	[trupo]
stable	**écurie** (f)	[ekyri]
pigsty	**porcherie** (f)	[pɔrʃəri]
cowshed	**vacherie** (f)	[vaʃri]
rabbit hutch	**cabane** (f) **à lapins**	[kaban ɑ lapɛ̃]
hen house	**poulailler** (m)	[pulaje]

90. Birds

bird	oiseau (m)	[wazo]
pigeon	pigeon (m)	[piʒɔ̃]
sparrow	moineau (m)	[mwano]
tit	mésange (f)	[mezɑ̃ʒ]
magpie	pie (f)	[pi]

raven	corbeau (m)	[kɔrbo]
crow	corneille (f)	[kɔrnɛj]
jackdaw	choucas (m)	[ʃuka]
rook	freux (m)	[frø]

duck	canard (m)	[kanar]
goose	oie (f)	[wa]
pheasant	faisan (m)	[fəzɑ̃]

eagle	aigle (m)	[ɛgl]
hawk	épervier (m)	[epɛrvje]
falcon	faucon (m)	[fokɔ̃]
vulture	vautour (m)	[votur]
condor (Andean ~)	condor (m)	[kɔ̃dɔr]

swan	cygne (m)	[siɲ]
crane	grue (f)	[gry]
stork	cigogne (f)	[sigɔɲ]

parrot	perroquet (m)	[perɔkɛ]
hummingbird	colibri (m)	[kɔlibri]
peacock	paon (m)	[pɑ̃]

ostrich	autruche (f)	[otryʃ]
heron	héron (m)	[erɔ̃]
flamingo	flamant (m)	[flamɑ̃]
pelican	pélican (m)	[pelikɑ̃]

| nightingale | rossignol (m) | [rɔsiɲɔl] |
| swallow | hirondelle (f) | [irɔ̃dɛl] |

thrush	merle (m)	[mɛrl]
song thrush	grive (f)	[griv]
blackbird	merle (m) noir	[mɛrl nwar]

swift	martinet (m)	[martinɛ]
lark	alouette (f) des champs	[alwɛt de ʃɑ̃]
quail	caille (f)	[kaj]

woodpecker	pivert (m)	[pivɛr]
cuckoo	coucou (m)	[kuku]
owl	chouette (f)	[ʃwɛt]
eagle owl	hibou (m)	[ibu]

wood grouse	tétras (m)	[tetra]
black grouse	tétras-lyre (m)	[tetralir]
partridge	perdrix (f)	[pɛrdri]

starling	étourneau (m)	[eturno]
canary	canari (m)	[kanari]
hazel grouse	gélinotte (f) des bois	[ʒelinɔt də bwa]
chaffinch	pinson (m)	[pɛ̃sɔ̃]
bullfinch	bouvreuil (m)	[buvrœj]

seagull	mouette (f)	[mwɛt]
albatross	albatros (m)	[albatros]
penguin	pingouin (m)	[pɛ̃gwɛ̃]

91. Fish. Marine animals

bream	brème (f)	[brɛm]
carp	carpe (f)	[karp]
perch	perche (f)	[pɛrʃ]
catfish	silure (m)	[silyr]
pike	brochet (m)	[brɔʃɛ]

| salmon | saumon (m) | [somɔ̃] |
| sturgeon | esturgeon (m) | [ɛstyrʒɔ̃] |

herring	hareng (m)	[arɑ̃]
Atlantic salmon	saumon (m) atlantique	[somɔ̃ atlɑ̃tik]
mackerel	maquereau (m)	[makro]
flatfish	flet (m)	[flɛ]

zander, pike perch	sandre (f)	[sɑ̃dr]
cod	morue (f)	[mɔry]
tuna	thon (m)	[tɔ̃]
trout	truite (f)	[trɥit]

eel	anguille (f)	[ɑ̃gij]
electric ray	torpille (f)	[tɔrpij]
moray eel	murène (f)	[myrɛn]
piranha	piranha (m)	[piraɲa]

shark	requin (m)	[rəkɛ̃]
dolphin	dauphin (m)	[dofɛ̃]
whale	baleine (f)	[balɛn]

crab	crabe (m)	[krab]
jellyfish	méduse (f)	[medyz]
octopus	pieuvre (f), poulpe (m)	[pjœvr], [pulp]

| starfish | étoile (f) de mer | [etwal də mɛr] |
| sea urchin | oursin (m) | [ursɛ̃] |

seahorse	hippocampe (m)	[ipɔkɑ̃p]
oyster	huître (f)	[ɥitr]
shrimp	crevette (f)	[krəvɛt]
lobster	homard (m)	[ɔmar]
spiny lobster	langoustine (f)	[lɑ̃gustin]

92. Amphibians. Reptiles

| snake | serpent (m) | [sɛrpɑ̃] |
| venomous (snake) | venimeux (adj) | [vənimø] |

viper	vipère (f)	[vipɛr]
cobra	cobra (m)	[kɔbra]
python	python (m)	[pitɔ̃]
boa	boa (m)	[bɔa]

grass snake	couleuvre (f)	[kulœvr]
rattle snake	serpent (m) à sonnettes	[sɛrpɑ̃ ɑ sɔnɛt]
anaconda	anaconda (m)	[anakɔ̃da]

lizard	lézard (m)	[lezar]
iguana	iguane (m)	[igwan]
monitor lizard	varan (m)	[varɑ̃]
salamander	salamandre (f)	[salamɑ̃dr]
chameleon	caméléon (m)	[kameleɔ̃]
scorpion	scorpion (m)	[skɔrpjɔ̃]

turtle	tortue (f)	[tɔrty]
frog	grenouille (f)	[grənuj]
toad	crapaud (m)	[krapo]
crocodile	crocodile (m)	[krɔkɔdil]

93. Insects

insect, bug	insecte (m)	[ɛ̃sɛkt]
butterfly	papillon (m)	[papijɔ̃]
ant	fourmi (f)	[furmi]
fly	mouche (f)	[muʃ]
mosquito	moustique (m)	[mustik]
beetle	scarabée (m)	[skarabe]

wasp	guêpe (f)	[gɛp]
bee	abeille (f)	[abɛj]
bumblebee	bourdon (m)	[burdɔ̃]
gadfly	œstre (m)	[ɛstr]

| spider | araignée (f) | [arɛɲe] |
| spider's web | toile (f) d'araignée | [twal darɛɲe] |

dragonfly	**libellule** (f)	[libelyl]
grasshopper	**sauterelle** (f)	[sotrɛl]
moth (night butterfly)	**papillon** (m)	[papijɔ̃]
cockroach	**cafard** (m)	[kafar]
tick	**tique** (f)	[tik]
flea	**puce** (f)	[pys]
midge	**moucheron** (m)	[muʃrɔ̃]
locust	**criquet** (m)	[krikɛ]
snail	**escargot** (m)	[ɛskargo]
cricket	**grillon** (m)	[grijɔ̃]
lightning bug	**luciole** (f)	[lysjɔl]
ladybug	**coccinelle** (f)	[kɔksinɛl]
cockchafer	**hanneton** (m)	[antɔ̃]
leech	**sangsue** (f)	[sɑ̃sy]
caterpillar	**chenille** (f)	[ʃənij]
earthworm	**ver** (m)	[vɛr]
larva	**larve** (f)	[larv]

FLORA

tree	arbre (m)	[arbr]
deciduous (adj)	à feuilles caduques	[ɑ fœj kadyk]
coniferous (adj)	conifère (adj)	[kɔnifɛr]
evergreen (adj)	à feuilles persistantes	[a fœj pɛrsistɑ̃t]

apple tree	pommier (m)	[pɔmje]
pear tree	poirier (m)	[pwarje]
sweet cherry tree	merisier (m)	[mərizje]
sour cherry tree	cerisier (m)	[sərizje]
plum tree	prunier (m)	[prynje]

birch	bouleau (m)	[bulo]
oak	chêne (m)	[ʃɛn]
linden tree	tilleul (m)	[tijœl]
aspen	tremble (m)	[trɑ̃bl]
maple	érable (m)	[erabl]

spruce	épicéa (m)	[episea]
pine	pin (m)	[pɛ̃]
larch	mélèze (m)	[melɛz]

fir tree	sapin (m)	[sapɛ̃]
cedar	cèdre (m)	[sɛdr]

poplar	peuplier (m)	[pøplije]
rowan	sorbier (m)	[sɔrbje]

willow	saule (m)	[sol]
alder	aune (m)	[on]

beech	hêtre (m)	[ɛtr]
elm	orme (m)	[ɔrm]

ash (tree)	frêne (m)	[frɛn]
chestnut	marronnier (m)	[marɔnje]

magnolia	magnolia (m)	[maɲɔlja]
palm tree	palmier (m)	[palmje]
cypress	cyprès (m)	[siprɛ]

mangrove	palétuvier (m)	[paletyvje]
baobab	baobab (m)	[baɔbab]
eucalyptus	eucalyptus (m)	[økaliptys]
sequoia	séquoia (m)	[sekɔja]

95. Shrubs

| bush | buisson (m) | [bҷisɔ̃] |
| shrub | arbrisseau (m) | [arbriso] |

| grapevine | vigne (f) | [viɲ] |
| vineyard | vigne (f) | [viɲ] |

raspberry bush	framboise (f)	[frɑ̃bwaz]
blackcurrant bush	cassis (m)	[kasis]
redcurrant bush	groseille (f) rouge	[grozɛj ruʒ]
gooseberry bush	groseille (f) verte	[grozɛj vɛrt]

acacia	acacia (m)	[akasja]
barberry	berbéris (m)	[bɛrberis]
jasmine	jasmin (m)	[ʒasmɛ̃]

juniper	genévrier (m)	[ʒənevrije]
rosebush	rosier (m)	[rozje]
dog rose	églantier (m)	[eglɑ̃tje]

96. Fruits. Berries

fruit	fruit (m)	[frҷi]
fruits	fruits (m pl)	[frҷi]
apple	pomme (f)	[pɔm]
pear	poire (f)	[pwar]
plum	prune (f)	[pryn]

strawberry	fraise (f)	[frɛz]
sour cherry	cerise (f)	[səriz]
sweet cherry	merise (f)	[məriz]
grape	raisin (m)	[rɛzɛ̃]

raspberry	framboise (f)	[frɑ̃bwaz]
blackcurrant	cassis (m)	[kasis]
redcurrant	groseille (f) rouge	[grozɛj ruʒ]
gooseberry	groseille (f) verte	[grozɛj vɛrt]
cranberry	canneberge (f)	[kanbɛrʒ]

orange	orange (f)	[ɔrɑ̃ʒ]
mandarin	mandarine (f)	[mɑ̃darin]
pineapple	ananas (m)	[anana]
banana	banane (f)	[banan]
date	datte (f)	[dat]

lemon	citron (m)	[sitrɔ̃]
apricot	abricot (m)	[abriko]
peach	pêche (f)	[pɛʃ]

| kiwi | kiwi (m) | [kiwi] |
| grapefruit | pamplemousse (m) | [pɑ̃pləmus] |

berry	baie (f)	[bɛ]
berries	baies (f pl)	[bɛ]
cowberry	airelle (f) rouge	[ɛrɛl ruʒ]
field strawberry	fraise (f) des bois	[frɛz de bwa]
bilberry	myrtille (f)	[mirtij]

97. Flowers. Plants

| flower | fleur (f) | [flœr] |
| bouquet (of flowers) | bouquet (m) | [bukɛ] |

rose (flower)	rose (f)	[roz]
tulip	tulipe (f)	[tylip]
carnation	oeillet (m)	[œjɛ]
gladiolus	glaïeul (m)	[glajœl]

cornflower	bleuet (m)	[bløɛ]
bluebell	campanule (f)	[kɑ̃panyl]
dandelion	dent-de-lion (f)	[dɑ̃dəljɔ̃]
camomile	marguerite (f)	[margərit]

aloe	aloès (m)	[alɔɛs]
cactus	cactus (m)	[kaktys]
rubber plant, ficus	ficus (m)	[fikys]

lily	lis (m)	[li]
geranium	géranium (m)	[ʒeranjɔm]
hyacinth	jacinthe (f)	[ʒasɛ̃t]

mimosa	mimosa (m)	[mimɔza]
narcissus	jonquille (f)	[ʒɔ̃kij]
nasturtium	capucine (f)	[kapysin]

orchid	orchidée (f)	[ɔrkide]
peony	pivoine (f)	[pivwan]
violet	violette (f)	[vjɔlɛt]

pansy	pensée (f)	[pɑ̃se]
forget-me-not	myosotis (m)	[mjɔzɔtis]
daisy	pâquerette (f)	[pɑkrɛt]

poppy	coquelicot (m)	[kɔkliko]
hemp	chanvre (m)	[ʃɑ̃vr]
mint	menthe (f)	[mɑ̃t]

| lily of the valley | muguet (m) | [mygɛ] |
| snowdrop | perce-neige (f) | [pɛrsənɛʒ] |

nettle	**ortie** (f)	[ɔrti]
sorrel	**oseille** (f)	[ozɛj]
water lily	**nénuphar** (m)	[nenyfar]
fern	**fougère** (f)	[fuʒɛr]
lichen	**lichen** (m)	[likɛn]
greenhouse (tropical ~)	**serre** (f) **tropicale**	[sɛr trɔpikal]
lawn	**gazon** (m)	[gazɔ̃]
flowerbed	**parterre** (m) **de fleurs**	[partɛr də flœr]
plant	**plante** (f)	[plɑ̃t]
grass	**herbe** (f)	[ɛrb]
blade of grass	**brin** (m) **d'herbe**	[brɛ̃ dɛrb]
leaf	**feuille** (f)	[fœj]
petal	**pétale** (m)	[petal]
stem	**tige** (f)	[tiʒ]
tuber	**tubercule** (m)	[tybɛrkyl]
young plant (shoot)	**pousse** (f)	[pus]
thorn	**épine** (f)	[epin]
to blossom (vi)	**fleurir** (vi)	[flœrir]
to fade, to wither	**se faner** (vp)	[sə fane]
smell (odor)	**odeur** (f)	[ɔdœr]
to cut (flowers)	**couper** (vt)	[kupe]
to pick (a flower)	**cueillir** (vt)	[kœjir]

98. Cereals, grains

grain	**grains** (m pl)	[grɛ̃]
cereal crops	**céréales** (f pl)	[sereal]
ear (of barley, etc.)	**épi** (m)	[epi]
wheat	**blé** (m)	[ble]
rye	**seigle** (m)	[sɛgl]
oats	**avoine** (f)	[avwan]
millet	**millet** (m)	[mijɛ]
barley	**orge** (f)	[ɔrʒ]
corn	**maïs** (m)	[mais]
rice	**riz** (m)	[ri]
buckwheat	**sarrasin** (m)	[sarazɛ̃]
pea plant	**pois** (m)	[pwa]
kidney bean	**haricot** (m)	[ariko]
soy	**soja** (m)	[sɔʒa]
lentil	**lentille** (f)	[lɑ̃tij]

T&P Books Publishing

Afghanistan	**Afghanistan** (m)	[afganistã]
Albania	**Albanie** (f)	[albani]
Argentina	**Argentine** (f)	[arʒãtin]
Armenia	**Arménie** (f)	[armeni]
Australia	**Australie** (f)	[ostrali]
Austria	**Autriche** (f)	[otriʃ]
Azerbaijan	**Azerbaïdjan** (m)	[azɛrbajdʒã]
The Bahamas	**Bahamas** (f pl)	[baamas]
Bangladesh	**Bangladesh** (m)	[bãgladɛʃ]
Belarus	**Biélorussie** (f)	[bjelɔrysi]
Belgium	**Belgique** (f)	[bɛlʒik]
Bolivia	**Bolivie** (f)	[bɔlivi]
Bosnia and Herzegovina	**Bosnie** (f)	[bɔsni]
Brazil	**Brésil** (m)	[brezil]
Bulgaria	**Bulgarie** (f)	[bylgari]
Cambodia	**Cambodge** (m)	[kãbɔdʒ]
Canada	**Canada** (m)	[kanada]
Chile	**Chili** (m)	[ʃili]
China	**Chine** (f)	[ʃin]
Colombia	**Colombie** (f)	[kɔlõbi]
Croatia	**Croatie** (f)	[krɔasi]
Cuba	**Cuba** (f)	[kyba]
Cyprus	**Chypre** (m)	[ʃipr]
Czech Republic	**République** (f) **Tchèque**	[repyblik tʃɛk]
Denmark	**Danemark** (m)	[danmark]
Dominican Republic	**République** (f) **Dominicaine**	[repyblik dɔminikɛn]
Ecuador	**Équateur** (m)	[ekwatœr]
Egypt	**Égypte** (f)	[eʒipt]
England	**Angleterre** (f)	[ãgletɛr]
Estonia	**Estonie** (f)	[ɛstɔni]
Finland	**Finlande** (f)	[fɛ̃lãd]
France	**France** (f)	[frãs]
French Polynesia	**Polynésie** (f) **Française**	[pɔlinezi frãsɛz]
Georgia	**Géorgie** (f)	[ʒeɔrʒi]
Germany	**Allemagne** (f)	[almaɲ]
Ghana	**Ghana** (m)	[gana]
Great Britain	**Grande-Bretagne** (f)	[grãdbrətaɲ]
Greece	**Grèce** (f)	[grɛs]
Haiti	**Haïti** (m)	[aiti]
Hungary	**Hongrie** (f)	[õgri]

100. Countries. Part 2

Iceland	Islande (f)	[islɑ̃d]
India	Inde (f)	[ɛ̃d]
Indonesia	Indonésie (f)	[ɛ̃dɔnezi]
Iran	Iran (m)	[irɑ̃]
Iraq	Iraq (m)	[irak]
Ireland	Irlande (f)	[irlɑ̃d]
Israel	Israël (m)	[israɛl]
Italy	Italie (f)	[itali]
Jamaica	Jamaïque (f)	[ʒamaik]
Japan	Japon (m)	[ʒapɔ̃]
Jordan	Jordanie (f)	[ʒɔrdani]
Kazakhstan	Kazakhstan (m)	[kazakstɑ̃]
Kenya	Kenya (m)	[kenja]
Kirghizia	Kirghizistan (m)	[kirgizistɑ̃]
Kuwait	Koweït (m)	[kɔwɛjt]
Laos	Laos (m)	[laos]
Latvia	Lettonie (f)	[lɛtɔni]
Lebanon	Liban (m)	[libɑ̃]
Libya	Libye (f)	[libi]
Liechtenstein	Liechtenstein (m)	[liʃtɛnʃtajn]
Lithuania	Lituanie (f)	[litu̯ani]
Luxembourg	Luxembourg (m)	[lyksɑ̃bur]
Macedonia (Republic of ~)	Macédoine (f)	[masedwan]
Madagascar	Madagascar (f)	[madagaskar]
Malaysia	Malaisie (f)	[malɛzi]
Malta	Malte (f)	[malt]
Mexico	Mexique (m)	[mɛksik]
Moldova, Moldavia	Moldavie (f)	[mɔldavi]
Monaco	Monaco (m)	[mɔnako]
Mongolia	Mongolie (f)	[mɔ̃gɔli]
Montenegro	Monténégro (m)	[mɔ̃tenegro]
Morocco	Maroc (m)	[marɔk]
Myanmar	Myanmar (m)	[mjanmar]
Namibia	Namibie (f)	[namibi]
Nepal	Népal (m)	[nepal]
Netherlands	Pays-Bas (m)	[peiba]
New Zealand	Nouvelle Zélande (f)	[nuvɛl zelɑ̃d]
North Korea	Corée (f) du Nord	[kɔre dy nɔr]
Norway	Norvège (f)	[nɔrvɛʒ]

101. Countries. Part 3

Pakistan	Pakistan (m)	[pakistɑ̃]
Palestine	Palestine (f)	[palɛstin]

Panama	**Panamá** (m)	[panama]
Paraguay	**Paraguay** (m)	[paragwɛ]
Peru	**Pérou** (m)	[peru]
Poland	**Pologne** (f)	[pɔlɔɲ]
Portugal	**Portugal** (m)	[pɔrtygal]
Romania	**Roumanie** (f)	[rumani]
Russia	**Russie** (f)	[rysi]

Saudi Arabia	**Arabie** (f) **Saoudite**	[arabi saudit]
Scotland	**Écosse** (f)	[ekɔs]
Senegal	**Sénégal** (m)	[senegal]
Serbia	**Serbie** (f)	[sɛrbi]
Slovakia	**Slovaquie** (f)	[slɔvaki]
Slovenia	**Slovénie** (f)	[slɔveni]

South Africa	**République** (f) **Sud-africaine**	[repyblik sydafrikɛn]
South Korea	**Corée** (f) **du Sud**	[kɔre dy syd]
Spain	**Espagne** (f)	[ɛspaɲ]
Suriname	**Surinam** (m)	[syrinam]
Sweden	**Suède** (f)	[sɥɛd]
Switzerland	**Suisse** (f)	[sɥis]
Syria	**Syrie** (f)	[siri]

Taiwan	**Taïwan** (m)	[tajwan]
Tajikistan	**Tadjikistan** (m)	[tadʒikistã]
Tanzania	**Tanzanie** (f)	[tãzani]
Tasmania	**Tasmanie** (f)	[tasmani]
Thailand	**Thaïlande** (f)	[tajlãd]
Tunisia	**Tunisie** (f)	[tynizi]
Turkey	**Turquie** (f)	[tyrki]
Turkmenistan	**Turkménistan** (m)	[tyrkmenistã]

Ukraine	**Ukraine** (f)	[ykrɛn]
United Arab Emirates	**Fédération** (f) **des Émirats Arabes Unis**	[federasjɔ̃ dezemira arabzyni]
United States of America	**les États Unis**	[lezeta zyni]
Uruguay	**Uruguay** (m)	[yrygwɛ]
Uzbekistan	**Ouzbékistan** (m)	[uzbekistã]

Vatican	**Vatican** (m)	[vatikã]
Venezuela	**Venezuela** (f)	[venezɥela]
Vietnam	**Vietnam** (m)	[vjɛtnam]
Zanzibar	**Zanzibar** (m)	[zãzibar]

T&P BOOKS

GASTRONOMIC GLOSSARY

This section contains a lot of words and terms associated with food. This dictionary will make it easier for you to understand the menu at a restaurant and choose the right dish

T&P Books Publishing

aftertaste	**arrière-goût** (m)	[arjɛrgu]
almond	**amande** (f)	[amɑ̃d]
anise	**anis** (m)	[ani(s)]
aperitif	**apéritif** (m)	[aperitif]
appetite	**appétit** (m)	[apeti]
appetizer	**hors-d'œuvre** (m)	[ɔrdœvr]
apple	**pomme** (f)	[pɔm]
apricot	**abricot** (m)	[abriko]
artichoke	**artichaut** (m)	[artiʃo]
asparagus	**asperge** (f)	[aspɛrʒ]
Atlantic salmon	**saumon** (m) **atlantique**	[somɔ̃ atlɑ̃tik]
avocado	**avocat** (m)	[avɔka]
bacon	**bacon** (m)	[bekɔn]
banana	**banane** (f)	[banan]
barley	**orge** (f)	[ɔrʒ]
bartender	**barman** (m)	[barman]
basil	**basilic** (m)	[bazilik]
bay leaf	**feuille** (f) **de laurier**	[fœj də lɔrje]
beans	**fèves** (f pl)	[fɛv]
beef	**du bœuf**	[dy bœf]
beer	**bière** (f)	[bjɛr]
beetroot	**betterave** (f)	[bɛtrav]
bell pepper	**poivron** (m)	[pwavrɔ̃]
berries	**baies** (f pl)	[bɛ]
berry	**baie** (f)	[bɛ]
bilberry	**myrtille** (f)	[mirtij]
birch bolete	**bolet** (m) **bai**	[bolɛ bɛ]
bitter	**amer** (adj)	[amɛr]
black coffee	**café** (m) **noir**	[kafe nwar]
black pepper	**poivre** (m) **noir**	[pwavr nwar]
black tea	**thé** (m) **noir**	[te nwar]
blackberry	**mûre** (f)	[myr]
blackcurrant	**cassis** (m)	[kasis]
boiled	**cuit à l'eau** (adj)	[kɥitalo]
bottle opener	**ouvre-bouteille** (m)	[uvrəbutɛj]
bread	**pain** (m)	[pɛ̃]
breakfast	**petit déjeuner** (m)	[pəti deʒœne]
bream	**brème** (f)	[brɛm]
broccoli	**brocoli** (m)	[brɔkɔli]
Brussels sprouts	**chou** (m) **de Bruxelles**	[ʃu də brysɛl]
buckwheat	**sarrasin** (m)	[sarazɛ̃]
butter	**beurre** (m)	[bœr]
buttercream	**crème** (f) **au beurre**	[krɛm o bœr]
cabbage	**chou** (m)	[ʃu]

cake	gâteau (m)	[gato]
cake	tarte (f)	[tart]
calorie	calorie (f)	[kalɔri]
can opener	ouvre-boîte (m)	[uvrəbwat]
candy	bonbon (m)	[bɔ̃bɔ̃]
canned food	conserves (f pl)	[kɔ̃sɛrv]
cappuccino	cappuccino (m)	[kaputʃino]
caraway	cumin (m)	[kymɛ̃]
carbohydrates	glucides (m pl)	[glysid]
carbonated	gazeuse (adj)	[gazøz]
carp	carpe (f)	[karp]
carrot	carotte (f)	[karɔt]
catfish	silure (m)	[silyr]
cauliflower	chou-fleur (m)	[ʃuflœr]
caviar	caviar (m)	[kavjar]
celery	céleri (m)	[sɛlri]
cep	cèpe (m)	[sɛp]
cereal crops	céréales (f pl)	[sereal]
cereal grains	gruau (m)	[gryo]
champagne	champagne (m)	[ʃɑ̃paɲ]
chanterelle	girolle (f)	[ʒirɔl]
check	addition (f)	[adisjɔ̃]
cheese	fromage (m)	[frɔmaʒ]
chewing gum	gomme (f) à mâcher	[gɔm a maʃe]
chicken	poulet (m)	[pulɛ]
chocolate	chocolat (m)	[ʃɔkɔla]
chocolate	en chocolat (adj)	[ɑ̃ ʃɔkɔla]
cinnamon	cannelle (f)	[kanɛl]
clear soup	bouillon (m)	[bujɔ̃]
cloves	clou (m) de girofle	[klu də ʒirɔfl]
cocktail	cocktail (m)	[kɔktɛl]
coconut	noix (f) de coco	[nwa də kɔkɔ]
cod	morue (f)	[mɔry]
coffee	café (m)	[kafe]
coffee with milk	café (m) au lait	[kafe o lɛ]
cognac	cognac (m)	[kɔɲak]
cold	froid (adj)	[frwa]
condensed milk	lait (m) condensé	[lɛ kɔ̃dɑ̃se]
condiment	condiment (m)	[kɔ̃dimɑ̃]
confectionery	confiserie (f)	[kɔ̃fizri]
cookies	biscuit (m)	[biskɥi]
coriander	coriandre (m)	[kɔrjɑ̃dr]
corkscrew	tire-bouchon (m)	[tirbuʃɔ̃]
corn	maïs (m)	[mais]
corn	maïs (m)	[mais]
cornflakes	pétales (m pl) de maïs	[petal də mais]
course, dish	plat (m)	[pla]
cowberry	airelle (f) rouge	[ɛrɛl ruʒ]
crab	crabe (m)	[krab]
cranberry	canneberge (f)	[kanbɛrʒ]
cream	crème (f)	[krɛm]
crumb	miette (f)	[mjɛt]

crustaceans	crustacés (m pl)	[krystase]
cucumber	concombre (m)	[kɔ̃kɔ̃br]
cuisine	cuisine (f)	[kɥizin]
cup	tasse (f)	[tɑs]
dark beer	bière (f) brune	[bjɛr bryn]
date	datte (f)	[dat]
death cap	oronge (f) verte	[ɔrɔ̃ʒ vɛrt]
dessert	dessert (m)	[desɛr]
diet	régime (m)	[reʒim]
dill	fenouil (m)	[fɵnuj]
dinner	dîner (m)	[dine]
dried	sec (adj)	[sɛk]
drinking water	eau (f) potable	[o potabl]
duck	canard (m)	[kanar]
ear	épi (m)	[epi]
edible mushroom	champignon (m) comestible	[ʃɑ̃piɲɔ̃ kɔmɛstibl]
eel	anguille (f)	[ɑ̃gij]
egg	œuf (m)	[œf]
egg white	blanc (m) d'œuf	[blɑ̃ dœf]
egg yolk	jaune (m) d'œuf	[ʒon dœf]
eggplant	aubergine (f)	[obɛrʒin]
eggs	les œufs	[lezø]
Enjoy your meal!	Bon appétit!	[bon apeti]
fats	lipides (m pl)	[lipid]
field strawberry	fraise (f) des bois	[frɛz de bwa]
fig	figue (f)	[fig]
filling	garniture (f)	[garnityr]
fish	poisson (m)	[pwasɔ̃]
flatfish	flet (m)	[flɛ]
flour	farine (f)	[farin]
fly agaric	amanite (f) tue-mouches	[amanit tymuʃ]
food	nourriture (f)	[nurityr]
fork	fourchette (f)	[furʃɛt]
freshly squeezed juice	jus (m) pressé	[ʒy prese]
fried	frit (adj)	[fri]
fried eggs	les œufs brouillés	[lezø bruje]
fried meatballs	boulette (f)	[bulɛt]
frozen	congelé (adj)	[kɔ̃ʒle]
fruit	fruit (m)	[frɥi]
fruits	fruits (m pl)	[frɥi]
game	gibier (m)	[ʒibje]
gammon	cuisse (f)	[kɥis]
garlic	ail (m)	[aj]
gin	gin (m)	[dʒin]
ginger	gingembre (m)	[ʒɛ̃ʒɑ̃br]
glass	verre (m)	[vɛr]
glass	verre (m) à vin	[vɛr ɑ vɛ̃]
goose	oie (f)	[wa]
gooseberry	groseille (f) verte	[grozɛj vɛrt]
grain	grains (m pl)	[grɛ̃]
grape	raisin (m)	[rɛzɛ̃]

grapefruit	pamplemousse (m)	[pɑ̃pləmus]
green tea	thé (m) vert	[te vɛr]
greens	verdure (f)	[vɛrdyr]
halibut	flétan (m)	[fletɑ̃]
ham	jambon (m)	[ʒɑ̃bɔ̃]
hamburger	farce (f)	[fars]
hamburger	hamburger (m)	[ɑ̃bœrgœr]
hazelnut	noisette (f)	[nwazɛt]
herring	hareng (m)	[arɑ̃]
honey	miel (m)	[mjɛl]
horseradish	raifort (m)	[rɛfor]
hot	chaud (adj)	[ʃo]
ice	glace (f)	[glas]
ice-cream	glace (f)	[glas]
instant coffee	café (m) soluble	[kafe sɔlybl]
jam	confiture (f)	[kɔ̃fityr]
jam	confiture (f)	[kɔ̃fityr]
juice	jus (m)	[ʒy]
kidney bean	haricot (m)	[ariko]
kiwi	kiwi (m)	[kiwi]
knife	couteau (m)	[kuto]
lamb	du mouton	[dy mutɔ̃]
lard	lard (m)	[lar]
lemon	citron (m)	[sitrɔ̃]
lemonade	limonade (f)	[limɔnad]
lentil	lentille (f)	[lɑ̃tij]
lettuce	laitue (f), salade (f)	[lety], [salad]
light beer	bière (f) blonde	[bjɛr blɔ̃d]
liqueur	liqueur (f)	[likœr]
liquors	boissons (f pl) alcoolisées	[bwasɔ̃ alkɔlize]
liver	foie (m)	[fwa]
lunch	déjeuner (m)	[deʒœne]
mackerel	maquereau (m)	[makro]
mandarin	mandarine (f)	[mɑ̃darin]
mango	mangue (f)	[mɑ̃g]
margarine	margarine (f)	[margarin]
marmalade	marmelade (f)	[marmәlad]
mashed potatoes	purée (f)	[pyre]
mayonnaise	sauce (f) mayonnaise	[sos majɔnɛz]
meat	viande (f)	[vjɑ̃d]
melon	melon (m)	[mәlɔ̃]
menu	carte (f)	[kart]
milk	lait (m)	[lɛ]
milkshake	cocktail (m) au lait	[kɔktɛl o lɛ]
millet	millet (m)	[mijɛ]
mineral water	eau (f) minérale	[o mineral]
morel	morille (f)	[mɔrij]
mushroom	champignon (m)	[ʃɑ̃piɲɔ̃]
mustard	moutarde (f)	[mutard]
non-alcoholic	sans alcool	[sɑ̃ zalkɔl]
noodles	nouilles (f pl)	[nuj]

oats	avoine (f)	[avwan]
olive oil	huile (f) d'olive	[ɥil dɔliv]
olives	olives (f pl)	[ɔliv]
omelet	omelette (f)	[ɔmlɛt]
onion	oignon (m)	[ɔɲɔ̃]
orange	orange (f)	[ɔrɑ̃ʒ]
orange juice	jus (m) d'orange	[ʒy dɔrɑ̃ʒ]
orange-cap boletus	bolet (m) orangé	[bɔlɛ ɔrɑ̃ʒe]
oyster	huître (f)	[ɥitr]
pâté	pâté (m)	[pate]
papaya	papaye (f)	[papaj]
paprika	paprika (m)	[paprika]
parsley	persil (m)	[pɛrsi]
pasta	pâtes (m pl)	[pat]
pea	pois (m)	[pwa]
peach	pêche (f)	[pɛʃ]
peanut	cacahuète (f)	[kakawɛt]
pear	poire (f)	[pwar]
peel	peau (f)	[po]
perch	perche (f)	[pɛrʃ]
pickled	mariné (adj)	[marine]
pie	gâteau (m)	[gato]
piece	morceau (m)	[mɔrso]
pike	brochet (m)	[brɔʃɛ]
pike perch	sandre (f)	[sɑ̃dr]
pineapple	ananas (m)	[anana]
pistachios	pistaches (f pl)	[pistaʃ]
pizza	pizza (f)	[pidza]
plate	assiette (f)	[asjɛt]
plum	prune (f)	[pryn]
poisonous mushroom	champignon (m) vénéneux	[ʃɑ̃piɲɔ̃ venenø]
pomegranate	grenade (f)	[grənad]
pork	du porc	[dy pɔr]
porridge	bouillie (f)	[buji]
portion	portion (f)	[pɔrsjɔ̃]
potato	pomme (f) de terre	[pɔm də tɛr]
proteins	protéines (f pl)	[prɔtein]
pub, bar	bar (m)	[bar]
pudding	pudding (m)	[pudiŋ]
pumpkin	potiron (m)	[pɔtirɔ̃]
rabbit	lapin (m)	[lapɛ̃]
radish	radis (m)	[radi]
raisin	raisin (m) sec	[rɛzɛ̃ sɛk]
raspberry	framboise (f)	[frɑ̃bwaz]
recipe	recette (f)	[rəsɛt]
red pepper	poivre (m) rouge	[pwavr ruʒ]
red wine	vin (m) rouge	[vɛ̃ ruʒ]
redcurrant	groseille (f) rouge	[grozɛj ruʒ]
refreshing drink	rafraîchissement (m)	[rafrɛʃismɑ̃]
rice	riz (m)	[ri]
rum	rhum (m)	[rɔm]

russula	russule (f)	[rysyl]
rye	seigle (m)	[sɛgl]
saffron	safran (m)	[safrɑ̃]
salad	salade (f)	[salad]
salmon	saumon (m)	[somɔ̃]
salt	sel (m)	[sɛl]
salty	salé (adj)	[sale]
sandwich	sandwich (m)	[sɑ̃dwitʃ]
sardine	sardine (f)	[sardin]
sauce	sauce (f)	[sos]
saucer	soucoupe (f)	[sukup]
sausage	saucisson (m)	[sosisɔ̃]
seafood	fruits (m pl) de mer	[frɥi də mɛr]
sesame	sésame (m)	[sezam]
shark	requin (m)	[rəkɛ̃]
shrimp	crevette (f)	[krəvɛt]
side dish	garniture (f)	[garnityr]
slice	tranche (f)	[trɑ̃ʃ]
smoked	fumé (adj)	[fyme]
soft drink	boisson (f) non alcoolisée	[bwasɔ̃ nonalkɔlize]
soup	soupe (f)	[sup]
soup spoon	cuillère (f) à soupe	[kɥijɛr ɑ sup]
sour cherry	cerise (f)	[səriz]
sour cream	crème (f) aigre	[krɛm ɛgr]
soy	soja (m)	[sɔʒa]
spaghetti	spaghettis (m pl)	[spagɛti]
sparkling	pétillante (adj)	[petijɑ̃t]
spice	épice (f)	[epis]
spinach	épinard (m)	[epinar]
spiny lobster	langoustine (f)	[lɑ̃gustin]
spoon	cuillère (f)	[kɥijɛr]
squid	calamar (m)	[kalamar]
steak	steak (m)	[stɛk]
stew	rôti (m)	[roti]
still	plate (adj)	[plat]
strawberry	fraise (f)	[frɛz]
sturgeon	esturgeon (m)	[ɛstyrʒɔ̃]
sugar	sucre (m)	[sykr]
sunflower oil	huile (f) de tournesol	[ɥil də turnəsɔl]
sweet	sucré (adj)	[sykre]
sweet cherry	merise (f)	[məriz]
taste, flavor	goût (m)	[gu]
tasty	bon (adj)	[bɔ̃]
tea	thé (m)	[te]
teaspoon	petite cuillère (f)	[pətit kɥijɛr]
tip	pourboire (m)	[purbwar]
tomato	tomate (f)	[tɔmat]
tomato juice	jus (m) de tomate	[ʒy də tɔmat]
tongue	langue (f)	[lɑ̃g]
toothpick	cure-dent (m)	[kyrdɑ̃]
trout	truite (f)	[trɥit]

tuna	**thon** (m)	[tɔ̃]
turkey	**dinde** (f)	[dɛ̃d]
turnip	**navet** (m)	[navɛ]
veal	**du veau**	[dy vo]
vegetable oil	**huile** (f) **végétale**	[ɥil veʒetal]
vegetables	**légumes** (m pl)	[legym]
vegetarian	**végétarien** (m)	[veʒetarjɛ̃]
vegetarian	**végétarien** (adj)	[veʒetarjɛ̃]
vermouth	**vermouth** (m)	[vɛrmut]
vienna sausage	**saucisse** (f)	[sosis]
vinegar	**vinaigre** (m)	[vinɛgr]
vitamin	**vitamine** (f)	[vitamin]
vodka	**vodka** (f)	[vɔdka]
waffles	**gaufre** (f)	[gofr]
waiter	**serveur** (m)	[sɛrvœr]
waitress	**serveuse** (f)	[sɛrvøz]
walnut	**noix** (f)	[nwa]
water	**eau** (f)	[o]
watermelon	**pastèque** (f)	[pastɛk]
wheat	**blé** (m)	[ble]
whisky	**whisky** (m)	[wiski]
white wine	**vin** (m) **blanc**	[vɛ̃ blɑ̃]
wine	**vin** (m)	[vɛ̃]
wine list	**carte** (f) **des vins**	[kart de vɛ̃]
with ice	**avec de la glace**	[avɛk dəla glas]
yogurt	**yogourt** (m)	[jaurt]
zucchini	**courgette** (f)	[kurʒɛt]

French-English gastronomic glossary

épi (m)	[epi]	ear
épice (f)	[epis]	spice
épinard (m)	[epinar]	spinach
œuf (m)	[œf]	egg
abricot (m)	[abriko]	apricot
addition (f)	[adisjõ]	check
ail (m)	[aj]	garlic
airelle (f) **rouge**	[ɛrɛl ruʒ]	cowberry
amande (f)	[amãd]	almond
amanite (f) **tue-mouches**	[amanit tymuʃ]	fly agaric
amer (adj)	[amɛr]	bitter
ananas (m)	[anana]	pineapple
anguille (f)	[ãgij]	eel
anis (m)	[ani(s)]	anise
apéritif (m)	[aperitif]	aperitif
appétit (m)	[apeti]	appetite
arrière-goût (m)	[arjɛrgu]	aftertaste
artichaut (m)	[artiʃo]	artichoke
asperge (f)	[aspɛrʒ]	asparagus
assiette (f)	[asjɛt]	plate
aubergine (f)	[obɛrʒin]	eggplant
avec de la glace	[avɛk dəla glas]	with ice
avocat (m)	[avɔka]	avocado
avoine (f)	[avwan]	oats
bacon (m)	[bekɔn]	bacon
baie (f)	[bɛ]	berry
baies (f pl)	[bɛ]	berries
banane (f)	[banan]	banana
bar (m)	[bar]	pub, bar
barman (m)	[barman]	bartender
basilic (m)	[bazilik]	basil
betterave (f)	[bɛtrav]	beetroot
beurre (m)	[bœr]	butter
bière (f)	[bjɛr]	beer
bière (f) **blonde**	[bjɛr blõd]	light beer
bière (f) **brune**	[bjɛr bryn]	dark beer
biscuit (m)	[biskɥi]	cookies
blé (m)	[ble]	wheat
blanc (m) **d'œuf**	[blã dœf]	egg white
boisson (f) **non alcoolisée**	[bwasõ nonalkɔlize]	soft drink
boissons (f pl) **alcoolisées**	[bwasõ alkɔlize]	liquors
bolet (m) **bai**	[bɔlɛ bɛ]	birch bolete

bolet (m) **orangé**	[bɔlɛ ɔrɑ̃ʒe]	orange-cap boletus
bon (adj)	[bõ]	tasty
Bon appétit!	[bɔn apeti]	Enjoy your meal!
bonbon (m)	[bõbõ]	candy
bouillie (f)	[buji]	porridge
bouillon (m)	[bujõ]	clear soup
boulette (f)	[bulɛt]	fried meatballs
brème (f)	[brɛm]	bream
brochet (m)	[brɔʃɛ]	pike
brocoli (m)	[brɔkɔli]	broccoli
cèpe (m)	[sɛp]	cep
céleri (m)	[sɛlri]	celery
céréales (f pl)	[sereal]	cereal crops
cacahuète (f)	[kakawɛt]	peanut
café (m)	[kafe]	coffee
café (m) **au lait**	[kafe o lɛ]	coffee with milk
café (m) **noir**	[kafe nwar]	black coffee
café (m) **soluble**	[kafe sɔlybl]	instant coffee
calamar (m)	[kalamar]	squid
calorie (f)	[kalɔri]	calorie
canard (m)	[kanar]	duck
canneberge (f)	[kanbɛrʒ]	cranberry
cannelle (f)	[kanɛl]	cinnamon
cappuccino (m)	[kaputʃino]	cappuccino
carotte (f)	[karɔt]	carrot
carpe (f)	[karp]	carp
carte (f)	[kart]	menu
carte (f) **des vins**	[kart de vɛ̃]	wine list
cassis (m)	[kasis]	blackcurrant
caviar (m)	[kavjar]	caviar
cerise (f)	[seriz]	sour cherry
champagne (m)	[ʃɑ̃paɲ]	champagne
champignon (m)	[ʃɑ̃piɲõ]	mushroom
champignon (m) **comestible**	[ʃɑ̃piɲõ kɔmɛstibl]	edible mushroom
champignon (m) **vénéneux**	[ʃɑ̃piɲõ venenø]	poisonous mushroom
chaud (adj)	[ʃo]	hot
chocolat (m)	[ʃɔkɔla]	chocolate
chou (m)	[ʃu]	cabbage
chou (m) **de Bruxelles**	[ʃu də brysɛl]	Brussels sprouts
chou-fleur (m)	[ʃuflœr]	cauliflower
citron (m)	[sitrõ]	lemon
clou (m) **de girofle**	[klu də ʒirɔfl]	cloves
cocktail (m)	[kɔktɛl]	cocktail
cocktail (m) **au lait**	[kɔktɛl o lɛ]	milkshake
cognac (m)	[kɔɲak]	cognac
concombre (m)	[kõkõbr]	cucumber
condiment (m)	[kõdimɑ̃]	condiment
confiserie (f)	[kõfizri]	confectionery
confiture (f)	[kõfityr]	jam
confiture (f)	[kõfityr]	jam

congelé (adj)	[kɔ̃ʒle]	frozen
conserves (f pl)	[kɔ̃sɛrv]	canned food
coriandre (m)	[kɔrjɑ̃dr]	coriander
courgette (f)	[kurʒɛt]	zucchini
couteau (m)	[kuto]	knife
crème (f)	[krɛm]	cream
crème (f) aigre	[krɛm ɛgr]	sour cream
crème (f) au beurre	[krɛm o bœr]	buttercream
crabe (m)	[krab]	crab
crevette (f)	[krəvɛt]	shrimp
crustacés (m pl)	[krystase]	crustaceans
cuillère (f)	[kɥijɛr]	spoon
cuillère (f) à soupe	[kɥijɛr a sup]	soup spoon
cuisine (f)	[kɥizin]	cuisine
cuisse (f)	[kɥis]	gammon
cuit à l'eau (adj)	[kɥitalo]	boiled
cumin (m)	[kymɛ̃]	caraway
cure-dent (m)	[kyrdɑ̃]	toothpick
déjeuner (m)	[deʒœne]	lunch
dîner (m)	[dine]	dinner
datte (f)	[dat]	date
dessert (m)	[desɛr]	dessert
dinde (f)	[dɛ̃d]	turkey
du bœuf	[dy bœf]	beef
du mouton	[dy mutɔ̃]	lamb
du porc	[dy pɔr]	pork
du veau	[dy vo]	veal
eau (f)	[o]	water
eau (f) minérale	[o mineral]	mineral water
eau (f) potable	[o potabl]	drinking water
en chocolat (adj)	[ɑ̃ ʃɔkɔla]	chocolate
esturgeon (m)	[ɛstyrʒɔ̃]	sturgeon
fèves (f pl)	[fɛv]	beans
farce (f)	[fars]	hamburger
farine (f)	[farin]	flour
fenouil (m)	[fənuj]	dill
feuille (f) de laurier	[fœj də lɔrje]	bay leaf
figue (f)	[fig]	fig
flétan (m)	[fletɑ̃]	halibut
flet (m)	[flɛ]	flatfish
foie (m)	[fwa]	liver
fourchette (f)	[furʃɛt]	fork
fraise (f)	[frɛz]	strawberry
fraise (f) des bois	[frɛz de bwa]	field strawberry
framboise (f)	[frɑ̃bwaz]	raspberry
frit (adj)	[fri]	fried
froid (adj)	[frwa]	cold
fromage (m)	[frɔmaʒ]	cheese
fruit (m)	[frɥi]	fruit
fruits (m pl)	[frɥi]	fruits
fruits (m pl) de mer	[frɥi də mɛr]	seafood
fumé (adj)	[fyme]	smoked

gâteau (m)	[gato]	cake
gâteau (m)	[gato]	pie
garniture (f)	[garnityr]	filling
garniture (f)	[garnityr]	side dish
gaufre (f)	[gofr]	waffles
gazeuse (adj)	[gazøz]	carbonated
gibier (m)	[ʒibje]	game
gin (m)	[dʒin]	gin
gingembre (m)	[ʒɛ̃ʒãbr]	ginger
girolle (f)	[ʒirɔl]	chanterelle
glace (f)	[glas]	ice
glace (f)	[glas]	ice-cream
glucides (m pl)	[glysid]	carbohydrates
goût (m)	[gu]	taste, flavor
gomme (f) à mâcher	[gɔm a maʃe]	chewing gum
grains (m pl)	[grɛ̃]	grain
grenade (f)	[grənad]	pomegranate
groseille (f) rouge	[grozɛj ruʒ]	redcurrant
groseille (f) verte	[grozɛj vɛrt]	gooseberry
gruau (m)	[gryo]	cereal grains
hamburger (m)	[ãbœrgœr]	hamburger
hareng (m)	[arã]	herring
haricot (m)	[ariko]	kidney bean
hors-d'œuvre (m)	[ɔrdœvr]	appetizer
huître (f)	[ɥitr]	oyster
huile (f) d'olive	[ɥil dɔliv]	olive oil
huile (f) de tournesol	[ɥil də turnəsɔl]	sunflower oil
huile (f) végétale	[ɥil veʒetal]	vegetable oil
jambon (m)	[ʒãbɔ̃]	ham
jaune (m) d'œuf	[ʒon dœf]	egg yolk
jus (m)	[ʒy]	juice
jus (m) d'orange	[ʒy dɔrãʒ]	orange juice
jus (m) de tomate	[ʒy də tɔmat]	tomato juice
jus (m) pressé	[ʒy prese]	freshly squeezed juice
kiwi (m)	[kiwi]	kiwi
légumes (m pl)	[legym]	vegetables
lait (m)	[lɛ]	milk
lait (m) condensé	[lɛ kɔ̃dãse]	condensed milk
laitue (f), salade (f)	[lety], [salad]	lettuce
langoustine (f)	[lãgustin]	spiny lobster
langue (f)	[lãg]	tongue
lapin (m)	[lapɛ̃]	rabbit
lard (m)	[lar]	lard
lentille (f)	[lãtij]	lentil
les œufs	[lezø]	eggs
les œufs brouillés	[lezø bruje]	fried eggs
limonade (f)	[limɔnad]	lemonade
lipides (m pl)	[lipid]	fats
liqueur (f)	[likœr]	liqueur
mûre (f)	[myr]	blackberry
maïs (m)	[mais]	corn
maïs (m)	[mais]	corn

mandarine (f)	[mɑ̃darin]	mandarin
mangue (f)	[mɑ̃g]	mango
maquereau (m)	[makro]	mackerel
margarine (f)	[margarin]	margarine
mariné (adj)	[marine]	pickled
marmelade (f)	[marməlad]	marmalade
melon (m)	[məlɔ̃]	melon
merise (f)	[məriz]	sweet cherry
miel (m)	[mjɛl]	honey
miette (f)	[mjɛt]	crumb
millet (m)	[mijɛ]	millet
morceau (m)	[mɔrso]	piece
morille (f)	[mɔrij]	morel
morue (f)	[mɔry]	cod
moutarde (f)	[mutard]	mustard
myrtille (f)	[mirtij]	bilberry
navet (m)	[navɛ]	turnip
noisette (f)	[nwazɛt]	hazelnut
noix (f)	[nwa]	walnut
noix (f) de coco	[nwa də kɔkɔ]	coconut
nouilles (f pl)	[nuj]	noodles
nourriture (f)	[nurityr]	food
oie (f)	[wa]	goose
oignon (m)	[ɔɲɔ̃]	onion
olives (f pl)	[ɔliv]	olives
omelette (f)	[ɔmlɛt]	omelet
orange (f)	[ɔrɑ̃ʒ]	orange
orge (f)	[ɔrʒ]	barley
oronge (f) verte	[ɔrɔ̃ʒ vɛrt]	death cap
ouvre-boîte (m)	[uvrəbwat]	can opener
ouvre-bouteille (m)	[uvrəbutɛj]	bottle opener
pâté (m)	[pɑte]	pâté
pâtes (m pl)	[pɑt]	pasta
pétales (m pl) de maïs	[petal də mais]	cornflakes
pétillante (adj)	[petijɑ̃t]	sparkling
pêche (f)	[pɛʃ]	peach
pain (m)	[pɛ̃]	bread
pamplemousse (m)	[pɑ̃pləmus]	grapefruit
papaye (f)	[papaj]	papaya
paprika (m)	[paprika]	paprika
pastèque (f)	[pastɛk]	watermelon
peau (f)	[po]	peel
perche (f)	[pɛrʃ]	perch
persil (m)	[pɛrsi]	parsley
petit déjeuner (m)	[pəti deʒœne]	breakfast
petite cuillère (f)	[pətit kɥijɛr]	teaspoon
pistaches (f pl)	[pistaʃ]	pistachios
pizza (f)	[pidza]	pizza
plat (m)	[pla]	course, dish
plate (adj)	[plat]	still
poire (f)	[pwar]	pear
pois (m)	[pwa]	pea

poisson (m)	[pwasɔ̃]	fish
poivre (m) noir	[pwavr nwar]	black pepper
poivre (m) rouge	[pwavr ruʒ]	red pepper
poivron (m)	[pwavrɔ̃]	bell pepper
pomme (f)	[pɔm]	apple
pomme (f) de terre	[pɔm də tɛr]	potato
portion (f)	[pɔrsjɔ̃]	portion
potiron (m)	[pɔtirɔ̃]	pumpkin
poulet (m)	[pulɛ]	chicken
pourboire (m)	[purbwar]	tip
protéines (f pl)	[prɔtein]	proteins
prune (f)	[pryn]	plum
pudding (m)	[pudiŋ]	pudding
purée (f)	[pyre]	mashed potatoes
régime (m)	[reʒim]	diet
rôti (m)	[roti]	stew
radis (m)	[radi]	radish
rafraîchissement (m)	[rafrɛʃismɑ̃]	refreshing drink
raifort (m)	[rɛfɔr]	horseradish
raisin (m)	[rɛzɛ̃]	grape
raisin (m) sec	[rɛzɛ̃ sɛk]	raisin
recette (f)	[rəsɛt]	recipe
requin (m)	[rəkɛ̃]	shark
rhum (m)	[rɔm]	rum
riz (m)	[ri]	rice
russule (f)	[rysyl]	russula
sésame (m)	[sezam]	sesame
safran (m)	[safrɑ̃]	saffron
salé (adj)	[sale]	salty
salade (f)	[salad]	salad
sandre (f)	[sɑ̃dr]	pike perch
sandwich (m)	[sɑ̃dwitʃ]	sandwich
sans alcool	[sɑ̃ zalkɔl]	non-alcoholic
sardine (f)	[sardin]	sardine
sarrasin (m)	[sarazɛ̃]	buckwheat
sauce (f)	[sos]	sauce
sauce (f) mayonnaise	[sos majɔnɛz]	mayonnaise
saucisse (f)	[sosis]	vienna sausage
saucisson (m)	[sosisɔ̃]	sausage
saumon (m)	[somɔ̃]	salmon
saumon (m) atlantique	[somɔ̃ atlɑ̃tik]	Atlantic salmon
sec (adj)	[sɛk]	dried
seigle (m)	[sɛgl]	rye
sel (m)	[sɛl]	salt
serveur (m)	[sɛrvœr]	waiter
serveuse (f)	[sɛrvøz]	waitress
silure (m)	[silyr]	catfish
soja (m)	[sɔʒa]	soy
soucoupe (f)	[sukup]	saucer
soupe (f)	[sup]	soup
spaghettis (m pl)	[spagɛti]	spaghetti
steak (m)	[stɛk]	steak

sucré (adj)	[sykre]	sweet
sucre (m)	[sykr]	sugar
tarte (f)	[tart]	cake
tasse (f)	[tɑs]	cup
thé (m)	[te]	tea
thé (m) noir	[te nwar]	black tea
thé (m) vert	[te vɛr]	green tea
thon (m)	[tɔ̃]	tuna
tire-bouchon (m)	[tirbuʃɔ̃]	corkscrew
tomate (f)	[tɔmat]	tomato
tranche (f)	[trɑ̃ʃ]	slice
truite (f)	[trɥit]	trout
végétarien (adj)	[veʒetarjɛ̃]	vegetarian
végétarien (m)	[veʒetarjɛ̃]	vegetarian
verdure (f)	[vɛrdyr]	greens
vermouth (m)	[vɛrmut]	vermouth
verre (m)	[vɛr]	glass
verre (m) à vin	[vɛr ɑ vɛ̃]	glass
viande (f)	[vjɑ̃d]	meat
vin (m)	[vɛ̃]	wine
vin (m) blanc	[vɛ̃ blɑ̃]	white wine
vin (m) rouge	[vɛ̃ ruʒ]	red wine
vinaigre (m)	[vinɛgr]	vinegar
vitamine (f)	[vitamin]	vitamin
vodka (f)	[vɔdka]	vodka
whisky (m)	[wiski]	whisky
yogourt (m)	[jaurt]	yogurt

* 9 7 8 1 7 8 4 9 2 4 5 9 1 *